LJC

Nov 96.

Apostasy   19
The Church's power to assimilate   36
Catholic worship, Protestants ["World Church!]   38
pure agnosticism   59
"The Cath. Ch. ... the only considerable religious
body that dares to claim an increasing & not a
diminishing membership" ...

Enlightment, Age of   79

The men of science   81
mind   131

papal headship of the ch.   178

THE QUOTABLE KNOX

THE
QUOTABLE
KNOX

A Topical Compendium of the Wit and Wisdom
of Ronald Knox

Edited by

GEORGE J. MARLIN, RICHARD P. RABATIN

and JOHN L. SWAN

Introduction by Monsignor Eugene V. Clark

IGNATIUS PRESS   SAN FRANCISCO

Cover art by Christopher J. Pelicano
Cover design by Riz Boncan Marsella

Our efforts are
dedicated
to

Monsignor Florence D. Cohalan,

Historian, Archdiocese of New York

and to

Joseph A. Bierbauer

1929–1989

CONTENTS

EDITORS' INTRODUCTION

What I have written does not belong to me. If I have written the truth, then it is "God's truth"; it would be true if every human mind denied it, or if there were no human minds in existence to recognize it. It is the obverse of that reality, that factualness, which belongs to some of our ideas and not to others; belongs to them, not in their own right—how could it?—but as lent to them by you, who are the focus and the background of all existence. If I have written well, that is not because Hobbs, Nobbs, Noakes and Stokes unite in praising it, but because it contains that interior excellence which is some strange refraction of your own perfect beauty; and of that excellence you alone are the judge. If it proves useful to others, that is because you have seen fit to make use of it as a weak tool, to achieve something in them of that supernatural end which is their destiny, and your secret.

These words of Ronald Knox, discovered after his death, were to be part of a preface to an unfinished work of apologetics. Evelyn Waugh rightfully declared that they "may stand as the epitaph of his life's work".

Like G. K. Chesterton and Fulton Sheen, Knox was a champion of what T. S. Eliot called the "Permanent Things". Throughout his long career, this scholar, preacher, essayist, poet, and mystery writer always defended the common man against the elite's latest fads and vices.

This man, who brought the Vulgate to life for twentieth-century man, believed that effectively to combat the modernists one must merely "trust orthodox tradition to determine what he is to believe, and common sense to determine what is orthodox tradition". It is the hope of the editors that the quotations excerpted from Ronald Knox's works give the reader a sense of that orthodox Tradition.

We are grateful to the following for their support: Larry and Pat Azar, Monsignor Eugene V. Clark, Monsignor Florence Cohalan, Michael G. Crofton, Mike Long, Patrick Foye, Joe Mysak, Rev. George William Rutler, Thomas Walsh, and Msgr. John Woolsey. At The Port Authority of New York and New Jersey, particular thanks to John Haley, Paul Blanco, Frank Bruno, Lysa Meduri, Sheree Van Duyne and Jean Ruane for putting up with one of the editors.

George J. Marlin
Richard P. Rabatin
John L. Swan

The City of New York
May 24, 1996

9

INTRODUCTION

I am delighted to introduce Ronald Knox to those who do not know him. All my adult life he has been a private pleasure, a delight expected and delivered, a literary and higher satisfaction on which to reflect and be pleased.

He is a happy part of the intellectual and esthetic life of so many who love fine English prose; who rejoice in the *joie de vivre* that bursts suddenly from this hooded, diffident person; who discern the apostolic roots of a devotional life that steadied his easily injured person. His uncommon literary gifts, restricted social instincts, and unlimited imagination, his bouts with self-doubt and dejection were all carried nicely by his deep trust in Christ and the dignity of an honorable priest.

Ronald Arbuthnott Knox (1888–1957), son and grandson of evangelical Anglican bishops—true believers—was born into a family of uncommon brightness and scholarly gifts. His childhood was filled with profound goodness and enlivening opportunities to learn and imagine, memorize the best, and wrestle with intellectual puzzles. His niece wrote, "As for Ronnie, the little boy who had been asked at four years old what he liked doing and had replied, 'I think all day, and at night I think about the past,' was already a natural philosopher".[1] At six he wrote letters salted with Greek and Latin words. He attended Eton and Balliol College, by contemporary estimate the finest schools in England in the attention they gave to students.

These were his advantages, and not much was lost. But he did not live in secure circumstances. As a small boy he lost his mother; he lived in no great homes. His family had not enough money for his schools; he had to win scholarships to each. All his life he had to be careful of money, and he worked hard, young and old, not to burden anyone.

From childhood he loved Church life and normal religious practice, and long before he ever saw a ritual service, he came to love ritual because he felt every object associated with worship was sacred. As two brothers slipped into agnosticism, Ronald taught himself sharp distinctions that served him well. Early he distinguished ritual, theology, and faith as exercises of very different value. An irredeemable romantic in religious matters (he loved Bruges as Catholic and Robert Hugh Benson's novels), he rejoiced in a sceptical mind ever demanding clear, supported truth. He was wary of theo-

[1] Penelope Fitzgerald, *The Knox Brothers* (London: Coward, McCann and Geoghegan, 1977), p. 46.

logical vagueness and intellectual shortcuts. His biographer, Evelyn Waugh, wrote:

> Such temptations against the Faith as he suffered—and he was near despair in the year before his reception into the Catholic Church—were total. Either the whole deposit of Faith was divinely inspired and protected and developed under divine guidance, or it was false. He never saw it, as did many of the contemporaries with whom he now took issue, as the agglomeration of history and fable, of hints and shadows of Truth, of vestigial philosophic notions and dark superstitions from which anyone could pick at will whatever he found agreeable, and discard the rest. He was for some years uncertain where he could find the authority which guarded and administered the Faith, but he always recognized it as a single, indivisible world.[2]

Nor did relaxing intellectually into the Faith diminish his sceptical approach to invention in Catholic doctrine and emotion-tinged theological conclusions. This was, of course, not the scepticism unbelievers proclaim but the mind of a clear-headed believer wanting to trust only purest apostolic teaching, and the longing of a scholar for clear, sure conclusions as a base for further reflection. Many other "truths" of religion he thought dangerous mush. One of his earliest pieces as an Anglo-Catholic was the often reprinted *Absolute and Abitofhell* (in the style of Dryden), in which he lampooned the waffling Anglican hierarchy. As an Anglican, early on, he saw that the first danger to the Church was not Protestantism, as most Anglo-Catholics thought, but modernism. Oddly, too, for an early ritualist, he considered the externals and consolations of religion very minor factors in spirituality. His sound thinking in this kept his sharp esthetic sense well grounded and also nicely liberated. He groaned inwardly at the wording of Catholic hymns and official prayers. But he never injured the feelings of those who profitted from those prayers.

Was it perhaps his demanding mind in limning the final verities that allowed him to abandon himself to comic devices in lectures and wild charades? He was so entertaining and delightful to high school girls that they were known to race home so as not to miss his talks. At Oxford he completed a lecture, offering his conclusions muffled in a gas mask.

One piece of doggerel will do:

> We love the pitch-pine pews
> On which our coat-tails bend,
> Designed to make us muse
> Upon our latter end.[3]

[2] Evelyn Waugh, *Ronald Knox* (London: Chapman Hall, 1959), p. 108.
[3] Waugh, p. 116.

After a long, painful wrestling with himself and grace and disbelief altogether, he submitted, exhausted and happy, to the Catholic Church on September 22, 1917.

He was ordained a Catholic priest on October 5, 1919.

It was no easy business for him. He enjoyed the finest education England had to offer, was well known as an Anglo-Catholic of lively positions and the author of very entertaining books, and was named the "wittiest young man in England" (*Daily Mail's Choice,* 1924). As he entered the Catholic Church and the priesthood, there were awkwardnesses and a few painful dislocations. He served as a master at Saint Edmund's Preparatory School and Seminary (1919–26) and as chaplain at Oxford (1926–39). Although his personality and learning, his hold on Christian doctrine and reality, his goodness and wit made a profound impression on many young people—mostly as they looked back—he knew he was painfully unsuited to the routine of those posts. He wrote and preached to larger congregations during his vacations, but he knew his literary work, of which so much was expected, was reduced to a thin stream of pleasant secondary works. (The exception was his brilliant *Let Dons Delight,* which appeared at the end of his Oxford chaplaincy.) At Saint Edmund's and Oxford we see the deeper "hidden stream" of his life: an honorable priest and self-denying Christian who had promised obedience to the Church and her work.[4] What is interesting is that he was ordained on his own "patrimony" (nonexistent), promising in effect to support himself and not to expect any pension. He supported himself largely by writing and preaching. Because of that circumstance, he could have removed himself from those two posts, but he accepted them for twenty years because the Church in the person of her hierarchy asked him to serve in them.

From 1939 to the last years of his life, he enjoyed chaplaincies in two accommodating English Catholic homes where he was a paying guest. In the first he was swallowed up in a girls' high school fleeing the bombing of London. He responded with the incisive and charming Slow Motion books for the girls on the Mass, Creed, and Gospels. They increase in popularity in our day.

But his two major works were also accomplished in that period. *Enthusiasm* (begun in 1919 and published in 1950) is his scholarly and enchanting exposition of the Christian religion, gone off the track of sound doctrine and sacramental life, turning into privately inspired and sometimes hilarious inventions. Serious students of Christianity cannot be without *Enthusiasm.* It is a truly insightful, sympathetic, and cool-eyed study of amazing Christians. And he also wrote his beautiful, graceful, and literarily inspired translation of

---

[4] "The Hidden Stream" was the title of a series of his lectures in which he developed an analogy between a stream now hidden under Oxford and the hidden sustaining Catholic Traditions of English Christianity.

the Bible during this period (1939–55). The Bible, on which people make such varied demands for clarity and mystery, mellifluousness and declarability, devotion and nostalgia, doctrine and more, cannot satisfy a majority through any one translation. But, I dare say, if contemporary Christians love both a clear, understandable, easily comprehended, reliable translation of the New Testament and the graces of a master's fine rhythmic prose, they need to pray for a handsome reprinting of Ronald Knox's translation. It is a refuge from the bathos and awkwardness of many contemporary translations and from the taunting of believers by citing the "brothers and sisters of Christ". The Old Testament, touched by Monsignor Knox with a note of archaism, divides admirers into those who love it and those who wished he had not added even a slight archaic shade to the clarity and style that were his genius.

As you will see from the bibliography, his collection of talks, sermons, and letters constitutes a major part of his published works. They created a special genre of his thinking and style. Most of his sermons were carefully crafted conversations that he read in the pulpit, but somehow he made them seem like easy dinner conversation. It was an uncommon style for sermons, but it will surely last. Some of his most thoughtful and evocative sermons were obituaries of the great figures he had known. Many were Newmanesque, as he gently exposed the heart and aspirations of a subject.

This charming don also left us a delicious menu of delightful communications. In *Essays in Satire* he punctured the pretentions of the higher critics of the Bible through a study of Sherlock Holmes and a piece that "proved" Queen Victoria wrote *In Memoriam.* He reveled in the absurdities of early Anglican ecumenism and in much else to delight honest men and women who enjoy the human comedy in religious and scholarly life.

Let Dons Delight was recognized immediately as the work of a master of English styles and of the nuances of English politics and theology. It is a work of subtle wit and good fun: conversations in an Oxford common room, every fifty years, from the Armada to our own time. It is, of course, full of wisdoms and pathos of a deeper sort. It is, for Catholics, a sign of hope in education wherever it is appreciated or understood.

Let us think of this volume of quotations selected by George Marlin, Richard Rabatin, and Jack Swan as a kind of "Reader's Delight".

Ronald Knox died a good Christian and loyal priest. Fame meant little to him; he suffered a dreadful fear that he might not have done enough with what the Lord had given him. We, his heirs of lesser gifts, may think he was more concerned than he need have been. But let us do what he wanted and pray for him in gratitude for the treasures of perception, belief, and easy wit that he gave us—his own happy *traditio* of Catholic Faith and good fun.

Monsignor Eugene V. Clark, Ph.D.
Church of Saint Agnes, New York City

14

A

Abstractions

Abstractions are themselves the creatures of the mind; and if the mind itself were an abstraction, we should have no abstractions at all.

—*CAL,* 76

I have never seen how an abstraction could get the whiphand of the concrete.

—*DIF,* 152

Academics

There are few more comfortable lives than that of an unmarried Fellow at one of the grey-stone universities.

—*OCC,* 247

Advertising (Modern)

Venditation is the characteristic activity of our age. Ease of manufacture has led, long since, to over-production, each firm trying to produce a world-supply of its own goods, in the hope that its own goods will be bought in preference to those of its rivals. And now the harassed artificer, finding himself left with stocks of unsaleable goods on his hands, must run for aid to the advertiser, in the hope that he will be able to put things right. The advertiser began in a humble way, as a medium between consumer and producer, to signify where and at what price certain goods could be bought. When competition was in full swing he reaped a harvest by crying one man's goods against another's. Now he performs a still more important economic function by trying to persuade us that we ought to buy goods which as a matter of fact we do not need.

—BCM, 66

Opticians shout at us, to tell us that we are going blind, tooth-paste firms, that we are in the grip of pyorrhoea, memory-trainers, that we are in danger of losing our jobs; a categorical imperative that brooks no question tells us we ought to drink more milk (an under-consumed article in these days when children are rare), to eat more fruit, and to season the primitive meal with a suitable quantity of mustard. The perplexed consumer is almost driven to imagine that it is his duty to impair his eyesight in order that he may need more spectacles, and to fortify his digestion with ever larger doses of patent medicines, lest he should fail in his civic obligation of reducing the milk-surplus.

—BCM, 66–67

Age

We have to recognise that there is a crust of natural habit forming round our lives all the time, . . . which seems to be the real self, but is in truth an overlay. In old age we are terribly conscious of this; what we are saying is but the echo of what we were saying twenty years ago; our prejudices, our appreciations are a legacy from past years, . . . But in middle life we are less wise; we congratulate ourselves that we have settled down now, our habits are fixed; we have thrown the passions of youth out of doors, and locked up the house. We forget that those would-be squatters have the latch-key, and are ready to return, more formidable than ever. Unless, of course, the house is tenanted by the love of God; merely garnished by self-conceit, it is to let with vacant possession.

—LIG, 38

America and Satire

No country, I suppose, has greater need of a satirist to-day than the United
States of America; no country has a greater output of humour, good and bad,
which is wholly devoid of any satirical quality. If a great American satirist
should arise, would his voice be heard among the hearty guffaws which are
dismally and eternally provoked by Mutt, Jeff, Felix, and other kindred
abominations?

—*ESS*, 42

Anglicanism

Anglicanism, generally speaking, is not a system of religion nor a body of
truth, but a feeling, a tradition, its roots intertwined with associations of
national history and of family life; you do not learn it, you grow into it; you
do not forget it, you grow out of it.

—*SPI*, 18

The Anglicanism of to-day, except where it is expounded by people definitely
under the influence of the Oxford movement, simply does not possess enough
of fixed background to allow of its being intelligently yet authoritatively
taught. The nature of God, the position and destiny of man, the meaning of
terms such as "soul" and "spirit"—fundamental doctrines such as these, with
no suggestion of "Romanism" about them, are subjects on which expert
Anglicans would pronounce variously, and non-expert Anglicans. . . . would
not pronounce at all. The idea of some schoolmasters I have known being
called upon to teach such doctrines according to a syllabus is not within the
bounds of moral possibility.

—*SPI*, 23

How long will it be before the Church of England loses its faith?

—*UAS*, 459

Roman Catholics have always been able to appeal to the traditions of our holy
Mother the Church. But the Church of England, as such, has nothing to
appeal to. How can we [Anglicans] pretend to appeal to Church tradition,

17

when we have cut ourselves off from the main stream of it, and any exposition of it must needs be a raking up of old dead documents, instead of obedience to a living voice? And how can we pretend to appeal to the Bible, when the Bible is for every man's private interpretation, and not expounded by authority?

—*UAS,* 459

Anglicans and Morals

You must have fixed standards . . . and they have none.

—*UAS,* 126

The Annunciation

The story of Paradise is repeating itself, but with variations; God, who once made a woman miraculously out of a man, is now making a Man miraculously out of a woman; and woman, whose disobedience was once the preface to man's rebellion against God, now, by her obedience, prefaces the perfect sacrifice of God made Man.

—*LAY,* 91

Anthropology

It is impossible to regard anthropology as a science in the strict sense; its theories will always be liable to revision.

—*BCM,* 73

Apathy

Hard hearts, not broken hearts, are the world's tragedy.

—*PAS,* 103

+ 1996 Re William Oddie, former Anglican par son, CofE fiddled with homosexuality, especially high Anglican seminaries. If all homosexual clergy were dismissed, the CofE would collapse

Apologists

It is very hard for the Catholic apologist nowadays to find a battle-ground where straight issues are to be fought; his opponents—that is, those who count—are usually content with a sneer here, an undocumented charge there, in the course of some treatise which has nothing ostensibly to do with religion; they do not trail their coats as of old.

—*DIF*, 240

Apostasy

People do go away from the Catholic Church. With the other Christianities, the line of division is perhaps not so clearly marked. . . . But the Catholic system, infinitely patient, infinitely gentle as it is to the consciences of waverers, has sharper edges, and people who lose direct contact with it are more tempted to react against it. . . . And the news of such a defection as that, even when there were circumstances to explain it, is—confess it—a tiny blow to your faith; a very gentle tap to test the stability of your own spiritual foundations. . . . Another's apostasy has cast a chill of loneliness over you.

—*PAS*, 322

We can only abandon the Catholic Church for some spiritual home which is more of a home than the Catholic Church. . . . Where are we to find such a revelation, such a spiritual home, such sources of inspiration? Nowhere; there is no other system in the world which dares even to claim what the Catholic Church claims. Are we to abandon the Catholic faith for something *less* than the Catholic faith?

—*PAS*, 323

Appetite

Wine, and the king, and women; those are crude terms under which the third book of Esdras would image for us three great appetites of our nature, the love of pleasure, the taste for power, the craving for human affection. To all those appetites we may have to say, "Get behind me", when the paramount claim of truth rules them out of consideration.

—*OCC*, 247

19

Aquinas, Saint Thomas

To hear the moderns talk, you would think that St. Thomas was a die-hard Conservative who could not rid his mind of the old Aristotelian way of thinking. Actually he was a daring innovator, who risked the charge of heresy in recalling us from a philosophy based on notions of the mind to a philosophy based on experience.... Yet this extraordinary man, in a short life of incessant literary activity, constructed and imposed on his generation a synthesis between philosophy and religion which his Arabian rivals failed, in the end, to secure for themselves. Christianity entered on a new world of speculation, while an Eastern rigidity numbed, and permanently, the thought of Islam.

—*GOD*, 23–24

Wherever you meet a man who professes interest in things of the mind, you will find that St Thomas means something to him. Possibly he will use the name "Aquinas" to indicate that this is not an author with whom he is on friendly terms; almost certainly he will admit that he has never tried to read "Aquinas". But there will be respect in his voice; he will know that he is referring, not to a medieval quibbler, but to an author whose works are one of the milestones in the history of human thought.

—*OCC*, 52

The Crusades were not yet over; we had not yet fought [the Muslims] to a standstill; but we had thought them to a standstill; nay, we had thought them back into the desert. And if we did that, if the Christian world did that, the praise is due, under God, to St. Thomas's fearless instinct that you must not be afraid of knowledge; that truth could not contradict truth, and whatever in Greek philosophy was true would harmonize with the Christian tradition; they would link together automatically, like St. Peter's chains.

—*OCC*, 55

Arches (Gothic)

Whatever you say in praise or dispraise of the Gothic, it has this claim at least on the gratitude of Christian people—it rests on the arch, the great pointed arch that is so apt a parable of the whole Christian idea. The arch, after all, is a kind of human miracle; its delicate shafts soaring upwards, and enabled by a feat of engineering to support a weight much heavier than themselves.

—*OCC*, 361

Arguments

To be present when two other people are arguing is, almost always, to be in a state of impotent fury at their joint incompetence.

—*DIF*, 260–61

Aristotle

St Thomas's thought is the unity of the sciences. It was a decisive moment in the world's history when St Albert and St Thomas, in defiance of so much nervous opposition, determined to make a Christian of Aristotle; Aristotle, the master-knower, the flower of pagan enlightenment. The Arabs had already adopted him, but they never made a Mohammedan of him. It is one of the most striking proofs of the superiority of Christianity to Islam, that when both tried the same philosophical diet we could digest it and they couldn't.

—*OCC*, 54–55

Arnauld, Antoine

He could bear anything except to be silenced.

—*EN*, 197

Art

A great picture, a great musical composition, a great book, but more than any of these, a great tragedy on the stage, affects you because it stands for a type of all the sorrows of the world, all the doubtful doom of human kind.

—*UAS*, 381

It is not easy; there would be no joy in art if the artist were not struggling with the limitations imposed on him by his materials. It means conforming to laws; no art has any meaning unless it conforms to laws.

—*UAS*, 364–65

Romeo and Juliet is not the tragedy of Romeo and Juliet, it is the eternal tragedy of blighted love. . . . *King Lear* is not the tragedy of King Lear, it is the eternal tragedy of man's ingratitude. Great art represents for us by a single instance, some eternal problem, some constantly repeated situation, and claims our tears not for this hero or heroine, not for this plot or this story, but for the eternal motive which underlies them all.

—*UAS*, 381

Artists

The artist loves his own work with a kind of parental affection; so much of himself has gone into it. Three separate facts—the author of the work, the work itself, the love of the author for his work. The work, a lifeless thing, cannot love in return. But the Expression of the Divine Artist's thought is as personal as himself, and the Love that passes between them is therefore mutual. And this Love itself is personal too; so Christian theology assures us. If the familiar formula "Father, Son and Holy Spirit" strikes us as barren of symbolic appropriateness, we can take refuge in the image of a Divine Mind with its Divine Thought, and a Divine Love which binds either of them to the other, and to itself.

—*LIG*, 70

The Ascension

As to the Ascension, I do not pretend to know whether a celestial body has weight, resistance, etc.; I do not know that Heaven was heavier after the Ascension, but I do know that earth was lighter.

—*SLS*, 221

Asceticism (Christian)

The aim of Christian asceticism is not to be without feelings, without preferences, without desires, like some Eastern fatalist. It is to subject our feelings, our preferences, our desires to the will of God by a continual peaceful act of aspiration to him. The perfect prayer is that in us and in all those we love, in those who wrong us, and in those whom we have scandalized or offended, in those whose lives are committed to our care, and in those who have asked us to pray for them, in all the beneficent economy of creation, and in all the varied events which distract the annals of human history, in the saints glorified in heaven, in the souls waiting in Purgatory, yes, even in the punishment of the lost, in life, in death, and in every creature, God's most high, most holy, and most adorable will may be done. It is the perfect prayer, covering and including all the minor petitions which human affection might suggest or human pity dictate to us; it puts the creature in its right relation to the Creator; it approaches most nearly, I suppose, to the prayer of the saints in heaven.

—*RFP*, 155

Atheism

Atheism is only a freak notion, cultivated by a few learned men.

—*HS*, 11

The argument against immortality isn't a piece of philosophical reasoning worked out by a set of deep thinkers in Moscow. It's a thing that naturally occurs to quite ordinary people like you and me when we wake up at four in the morning after a heavy dinner the night before.

—*HS*, 41

Atheism (Modern)

We are threatened by forces not less highly organized than in the days of the first persecutions; not less ruthless than the barbarians of the Dark Ages, not less fanatical than the storm-troops of the Reformation. The world at large is still indifferent to religion, as it was yesterday and the day before, and now stands stupefied at the appearance of a new philosophy which believes that religion matters, matters so intensely that it has got to be wiped out.

—*UAS*, 430–31

Atheists

And most of these people do not think about God if they can help it—that is what I call "forgetting God". They try to satisfy themselves with this world .... The man who confines his outlook to this world is worried all the time, at the back of his mind, by the old riddle of existence; the troubles, the sufferings, the tragedies of the world keep flicking him like briers as he goes along.

—*OCC*, 13

Why do we pray so often for the wanderers who are following a false path, so little for those who can find no path at all?

—*OCC*, 356

His judgment, like yours and mine, lies in God's hands; it is a small thing that he should be judged by our standards.

—*OCC*, 357

We ought to remember them as brothers of ours, deceived at the moment by a lie, but guilty in varying degrees, and those perhaps most needing our prayers, who are guiltiest. "I thought it my duty", says St Paul, and St Augustine reminds us that, as a rule, when we think we are hating an enemy, we are hating a brother without knowing it. Let us ask for all men the mercy we all need, and leave judgment in his hands, who alone can judge, who alone can punish.

—*OCC*, 358

We shall not begin to understand the attitude of the modern unbeliever towards the Church until we realize that he thinks of us as a conspiracy: a conspiracy to set up an unholy Roman Empire over the consciences of an enslaved race.

—*OCC*, 358

You have . . . passed such loiterers in the streets with mixed feelings of pity and contempt, marked how they seemed to converse but rarely . . . gazed vacantly at the stream of busy life that passed them by; and you have wondered how existence could be tolerable with so little of apparent purpose. And yet, look at your own record as you would look at it if you were told that the story of it was to close tomorrow: how much of it has more value for eternity than if your lot had been cast at the street corner?

—*PAS*, 143–44

Atom Bomb and Utopia

The men of our own age have been obsessed with the idea of a world in which freedom and common humanity were becoming, from century to century, more firmly established. But the advent of a new weapon, destructive on a scale hitherto unknown, seems to alter the whole perspective of historical probabilities; men who till yesterday were boldly prophesying a golden age are now wistfully hoping for it.

—*GOD*, II

Atonement

A. owes B. £500, and can't pay. C. offers to pay off the debt, and B. accepts the offer. What can A. do? He has ceased to be a debtor, whether he wanted to or not; the decision is not in his hands. So it is with our Lord's Atonement; it has been accepted on our behalf, and it is no good your bustling about saying you prefer to do things by your own effort. No effort you could possibly make would suffice as satisfaction for one mortal sin. All we can do is to unite our feeble efforts with the gratuitous merits of our Lord's Sacrifice, and ask God to accept them in that form.

—*OR*, 157

If we are to hold the full traditional view of the Atonement, we must suppose that the brand left by our sins is not twofold, but threefold. They leave a mark on our own souls—true. They leave a mark on the lives of men around us—true. But over and above all this, they leave a mark in the book of life, a black mark on our records, which no human penitence can efface.

—*SLS*, 170

Automobiles

The motor-car, in bringing us all closer together, by making it easy to have luncheon two counties away, has driven us all further apart, by making it unnecessary for us to know the people in the next bungalow. And so, once again, we have to thank civilisation for nothing.

—*BAR*, 196–97

+ whatever else a tower block is, it is most certainly not a community.

B

Bacon, Roger

Bacon was not much of a saint—he was more of a don. He had the don's unalterable conviction that all the other dons were going the wrong way about things.

—*OCC*, 158

Beauty and Love

That world into which Jesus Christ has ascended is not a world of shadows; it is a world of realities, which casts its shadows on earth. . . . Human love, human beauty, are only the shadow, not the substance. They could not move our natures so deeply, if they had not in them something of the divine; and yet, so imperfect, so fugitive, so unsatisfying, they can only be shadows. Somewhere, beyond the reach of our senses, there must be perfect love, perfect beauty, of which we can form no true idea—meanwhile, these blurred shadows are better than nothing.

—*OCC*, 306

Beggars

If ever there was a beggar, it was St Paul. You talk about the clergy always wanting money, but it is extraordinary how large a part of St Paul's writings refer directly to the Sunday collections. And I suppose it is probable that St Paul was criticized—whether by discontented Christians or by people outside the Church—for the persistent way in which he raised funds . . . to supply the needs of the Church at Jerusalem. And his answer was perfectly simple; "if we have sown unto you spiritual things, is it a great matter if we reap your carnal things?"[1]

—*PAS*, 192–93

Begging

The necessity of begging for your bread is a salutary form of humiliation. And again, the fact of not knowing where your next meal is to come from gives you a clear sense, very much to be desired but not easily attainable, of man's continual dependence upon the providence of almighty God.

—*PAS*, 193

Belief and Experience

If a man professes to accept any religious doctrine only or chiefly on that ground, claiming that he or any other man has "verified" it by "experience", meaning that he has tried the experiment of behaving as if that doctrine were true, and has found some kind of spiritual satisfaction in so doing, I say that is cant, and mischievous cant. Cant, because he is transferring a certainty which he only feels about his own states of mind to a reality lying outside of, and corresponding to, those states of mind, which is a vicious process. It proves nothing.

—*DIF*, 131

Belloc, Hilaire

Belloc wrote like an old man in his youth; just as Chesterton wrote like a boy in late life.

—*LIT*, 156

He belonged to that period, that culture, in which a receptive mind refreshed itself, almost unconsciously, at the spring of the Classics.

—*LIT*, 200

[1] 1 Cor 9.11.

What he cared for was not the good word of posterity taken in the gross, but the praise of Christendom.

—*OCC,* 410

A historian who had the rare quality of making the past live.

—*OCC,* 411

You do not often hear it said of Belloc, as you hear it said of Chesterton, "I owe my conversion to him". But the influence of a prophet is not to be measured by its impact on a single mind here and there; it exercises a kind of hydraulic pressure on the thought of his age. And when the day of wrath comes, and that book is brought out, written once for all, which contains all the material for a world's judgment, we shall perhaps see more of what Belloc was and did.

—*OCC,* 413

Benefactors

In our common experience, who is it that excites our dislike almost as much as the ungrateful man? Surely the benefactor who is always harping on his benefits and demanding gratitude.

—*PAS,* 221

The Bible

Indeed, it is doubtful whether we shall ever again allow ourselves to fall under the spell of a single, uniform text, consecrated by its antiquity.

—*TOT,* x

The Bible (Protestant vs. Catholic)

One of the leading differences between the Catholic and the Protestant Bibles is that the former gives 'do penance' (from *poenitentiam agere*) where the latter gives 'repent' (from *metanoein*). Rivers of ink flowed over the controversy; Catholic expositors were determined not to let it be supposed that sins were forgiven in return for a mere attitude of the mind, as opposed to a genuine alteration of the will.

— TOT, 78

Bible Translators

You see, it is no ordinary task. If you translate, say, the *Summa* of St. Thomas, you expect to be cross-examined by people who understand philosophy and by people who understand Latin; no one else. If you translate the Bible, you are liable to be cross-examined by anybody; because everybody thinks he knows already what the Bible means.

— TOT, 106

Bishops' Responsibilities

Who is to ensure that Catholic students, exposed to the influence of so many inadequate philosophies, are at the same time confronted, and effectively, with the eternal truths of religion? . . . it is the responsibility of the diocesan. They say that if you suffer from insomnia it is a good thing to lie in bed and count sheep jumping over a hedge. For some people perhaps it may be; but not, I think, for bishops.

— OCC, 353–54

The Blessed Mother and Protestants

Protestants sometimes laugh at us because we address ourselves, now to our Lady of Perpetual Succour, now to our Lady of Good Counsel, now to our Lady of Lourdes, and so on, as if they were so many different people. But the case is much worse than that, if they only knew; every individual Catholic has a separate our Lady to pray to, his Mother, the one who seems to care for him individually, has won him so many favours, has stood by him in so many difficulties, as if she had no other thought or business in heaven but to watch over him.

—RFP, 175

The Body

This body of yours, with whatever graces endow it, with all that it has attracted to itself of earth, is destined at last for the charnel-house. All of you that belongs to the body . . . strength of muscle, all that of your intellectual faculties, . . . all the charm you have for others, and the warm memories you have carried away of good days past—all *that* comes from dust and belongs to dust, and you must make your last journey without it. From dust we came, to dust we go; dust we are, unstable and worthless; let us get that into our heads.

—LAY, 18

Body and Mind

Man fell, and as the result of his fall the predestined union of body and soul could no longer be a union of happiness and peace. The soul, created in God's image, finds itself an uneven match for its material partner. Man is born at war with himself.

—RFP, 6

The Body and Soul

This body of yours *is you.* No good to talk, Eastern-fashion, as if the body were a cage in which your soul is imprisoned, or a garment which your soul wears and can slip off at any time. It is all very well as a matter of rhetoric to talk about your body as a garment of dust. But if somebody jabs a pin into you, it is no use telling yourself that it is going into your garment of dust; it goes into you. The liaison, whatever it be, between your body and your soul is something quite unique; we have no comparison, in the whole of our experience, which would begin to make it clearer to us.

—LAY, 14

Brotherhood of Man

The birth of a Saviour was not for the Jewish people only, it was for the whole world; all mankind became brothers when God became man. Always, in defiance of the probabilities, one of the three kings is represented as a native African; there should be no doubt that the Church was worldwide. The brotherhood of man. . . . Will it ever be achieved? . . . Christendom has never abandoned that idea, has fought for it, time and again, in face of man's obstinate tendency towards nationalism.

—PAS, 365

Buddhism

It is enough for us to reiterate that Christianity is something else besides mysticism, whereas Buddhism is precious little else.

—HS, 113

You must not be content to compare the Buddhist saint with the Christian saint; you must compare the Buddhist sinner with the Christian sinner. The religion of Christ is not only for those favoured souls who can manage to leave this earth on the wings of contemplation. It is for struggling souls too, all blinded by the blood and sweat of the world's conflict, half caught in the mire of its beastliness, and yet somehow keeping hold of that Christ who pardoned the adulteress, and saved his doubting apostle from being swallowed up by the waves.

—HS, 113–14

Bureaucracy and Statistics

Administrative Government by counting of heads is liable to abuse; the investigation of facts by counting of heads is, from the outset, a preposterous form of procedure.

—SLS, 175

C

Calvary

There was no spectator at the death on Calvary, however casual, however insignificant, that did not carry away in his heart the seed of life or of death. There has been and will be no human creature who, when the last sheaf is bound and the last load garnered, will not be found to have accepted or refused that seed of life, and in accepting or refusing it signed the warrant of its own eternal destiny.

—PAS, 150

Bethlehem means Christ born in man, and man re-born in Christ. Calvary means that mankind has died in the person of Christ, it means also that Christ has died in the name of mankind; not instead of us, as our substitute, but in our name as our representative.

—PAS, 509

Campion, Saint Edmund

There, he is quite unlike Newman; Newman sees the other man's point of view almost better than he sees his own. Even when he is being interrogated by his judges, or browbeaten by Protestant theologians, men briefed to put the Government's case, you feel Campion is wondering all the time how on earth they can manage to be so dense about it.

—OCC, 138

33

Catholicism

The difficulties people find in accepting the Catholic position are not entirely of our making. Assuredly there is no institution in the world whose enemies have mugged up their brief against it so carefully, dragging to light every circumstance which could discredit it, and occasionally, with varying degrees of excuse, just lying about it.

—*DIF,* 215

The world does still hate Catholicism.

—*PAS,* 157

The Catholic religion is very much more than a creed; it is a life, a warfare, a loyalty, a romance. But it is a creed too; and the assertion of it involves us in an intellectual responsibility. Man's intellect is part of himself, and must be represented, consequently, in the scheme of his salvation.

—*PAS,* 184

The Catholic Church is only just beginning. The movements of history that pass and repass, chequering her sunshine with shadow, they are only the clouds of early morning for all we know. . . . we have passed through darker hours than this. . . . if the hatred or the contempt of men could kill the Catholic faith, it would have been dead long ago.

—*UAS,* 361

Catholicism and the Christianities

Oh, we are a convenience to the other Christianities, we Catholics; a lightning-conductor to draw the world's criticism away from them; a repository whose furniture they can reproduce without the worm-holes; a standard of theological currency, against which they can balance their rate of exchange. . . . Our whole witness is stultified if we are not to be the absolute thing we claim to be.

—*DIF,* 214

34

Catholic Persecution

We cannot expect to live much longer under the shadow of the other Christianities; as time goes on, we shall have to face, more and more, the glare of the world's hostility. For that reason, we must rally closer than ever round our bishops, our clergy, our churches, our schools; we must be active Catholics, instructed Catholics, if need be combative Catholics, to meet the demands of the new age.

—*OCC,* 181

Catholics

In English life the non-Catholic churchgoer is normally . . . the kind of steady-going person who takes no risks, and does not run up much against temptations. Whereas Catholics take risks, . . . they are always well represented in what Puritanism regards as the risky professions, the turf, the stage, the ring, and so on. The crowd they live with is often a crowd which has precious little morals, and yet it does not seem to touch them.

—*DIF,* 198

There is a tendency, somehow, to treat a Catholic as a different kind of animal; and in a vague way feel as if it were all right for *him* to believe these things. As if it could ever be right to believe what is untrue, or as if it were possible for a thing to be true for one person and not for another!

—*HS,* 17

Say what you will, the other Christianities are so hall-marked with their place of origin, reflect so perfectly a German, or an English, or an American outlook; even their virtues are so much the characteristic virtues of a particular and rather modern culture, that you can't think of their missionary influence, splendid as it often is, as a Catholicizing influence. Whatever else they dislike about us, men admire, and envy, our international ubiquity.

—*HS,* 120

The point about the Church is that she has the power to assimilate, to digest, fresh ideas, instead of merely gulping them down; all her history makes us sure of that. And in that power of assimilation, she is Catholic.

—*HS*, 122

The world knows that Catholics have a high standard of purity. But the world is not going to be impressed unless it is assured that Catholics keep it.

—*OCC*, 9

Each of us, whether he likes it or not, is an advertisement of the Catholic faith to the little circle of his neighbours—a good advertisement, or a bad advertisement. And it is such a mistake to think that we ought to try and impress our neighbours by making it clear to them that Catholics are not Puritans, are not strait-laced, are sportsmen like anybody else.

—*OCC*, 9

The difference between being merely Catholic by creed, and being a full citizen of the Catholic world, in times like these, is, if I may degrade the subject by an undignified metaphor, all the difference between merely watching a race and watching a race you have money on.

—*OCC*, 217

A hundred years ago our enemies blamed us for thinking wrong; today they blame us for thinking. They hustle the unwelcome metaphysician into the concentration camp, into the gas-chamber.

—*OCC*, 250

Every Catholic is to some extent a marked man; in the casual contacts of daily life he is bearing witness, or failing to bear witness, to Jesus Christ. . . . the point is, not so much that we ought to be better Catholics, but that we ought to be better Christians. That we should be lovers of the truth, fair-minded, ready to believe the best of people, impatient of scandal, considerate towards the unbefriended, generous in our enthusiasms, temperate in our pleasures, discreet in our friendships, that we should have a smile for everybody—in a word, that we should live in the sunlight of that creed which we profess.

—OCC, 349

The world [will never] give a just hearing to one who has labelled himself a Catholic.

—OCC, 405

People laugh at the Puritan but they do not laugh at the Catholic, they feel they are up against something too hard and too formidable for that.

—UAS, 127

There's always a polite assumption nowadays that what one says about Catholics doesn't apply to any Catholic who may happen to be in the room—but you see, one can't *always* be in the room. And I think that we most of us have a thoroughly well-grounded suspicion that when our backs are turned our Protestant friends say: "Dear me, dear me, what a pity!"

—UAS, 354

Catholics (as Reformers)

For the whole of your lifetimes, probably, everything that we Catholics do or propose to do in that line will be viewed with suspicion, will be misrepresented; we shall be told that we are only half-hearted reformers, trying to take the wind out of other people's sails. . . . we have got to work for the relief of human misery without defying the sanctities of the divine law. So we shall always be at a disadvantage compared with other reformers who can only see one set of principles at a time, and we shall get no thanks for our interference.

—UAS, 120

Catholics (Honorary)

It is not difficult to recognize in Herod a type of that curious class of people whom you can only call honorary members of the Catholic Church. They have never been received, and do not mean to be, but when they do go to church it is always to a Catholic church. They know all sorts of odd points of moral and devotional theology better than the ordinary Catholic. . . . But they are not Catholics; they are only cultured dabblers . . . and the crucial test comes to them when something strikes across their lives which forces them to be serious; a bad illness, or a severe bereavement . . . and the illness takes them to Christian Science, or the bereavement to Spiritualism, or the gust of passion blows them away altogether, but there is another seat empty at the eleven o'clock Mass.

—*PAS*, 158–59

Catholics vs. Protestants

If you get arguing with your non-Catholic friends about religion, you mustn't let them think that we Catholics differ from them over one or two additional points of doctrine which we believe and they don't, like indulgences or the infallibility of the Pope. The question over which we differ from them is a fundamental one, which precedes all other discussion. . . . We believe that the first requisite of the Christian vocation is to belong to a particular religious body, the religious body which is represented in England by the Cardinal Archbishop of Westminster. . . . If you don't belong to that body, it doesn't make the slightest difference whether you believe in indulgences, or the infallibility of the Pope, . . . mere believing won't help you, unless you enjoy or are prepared to accept, membership of the one visible Church of Christ.

—*ISG*, 80

Change

We are changing . . . all the time, ever so little; habits grow upon us, new interests grip us; how easy it is even after years of friendship to find that the other person is not quite what you thought he was—or is it that you are not quite what you thought you were? . . . an illusion has faded.

—*PAS*, 280

† Eẍct "the World Church", a quite fantastic myth that has existed₃₈ for at least a generation or two, & enables its adherents to call themselves Christians, while at one & the same believing almost anything or almost nothing.

Character

To be the artist of his own character, Man must have laws, outside of himself and higher than himself, to which he is to conform his operations. You may go further than that, and say that all art demands an ideal, an ideal which the artist wishes to translate into reality. A man, then, must have ideals to live by; he must want to translate those ideals into reality in his own character.

—*UAS*, 130

Charity

Charity edifies; recognizes that it has a duty to the souls of others.

—*EN*, 17

That spirit of charity which St Paul saw as the bond of Christian fellowship begins with you and me; begins in the diocese, in the parish, at the club, round the tea-table. It is a force which you and I, in our small way, can generate or fail to generate; in moments of careless gossip, when we malign, and criticize, and complain; in petty struggles for unimportant posts of leadership, in cabals and whispering campaigns. Talk, always, as you would talk if St Paul was in the room.

—*OCC*, 379

Charity towards complete strangers has become a habit with us. It has filled the world with hospitals and orphanages and almshouses, all because of Bethlehem; there was no name for such things before Jesus Christ came. Because Jesus Christ came to redeem us when we were strangers who had no claim on him, brought redemption to everybody far and near, we too, even you and I, are ashamed to button up our pockets.

—*PAS*, 367

Chesterton, Gilbert Keith

To me Chesterton's philosophy, in the broadest sense of that word, has been part of the air I breathed, ever since the age when a man's ideas begin to disentangle themselves from his education. His paradoxes have become, as it were, the platitudes of my thought. And this was a man whose genius touched everything.

—*LIT,* 155

It is probable that no article or essay on paradox will ever be written in which Chesterton is not mentioned, so much did he make the weapon his own.

—*LIT,* 156

Chesterton made us see the value of old institutions, the cogency of old truths, by dint of travelling round the world, as it were, to rediscover them—by reinterpreting truisms as the paradoxes they really were, things staled by familiarity as the exciting, adventurous things they really were. Chesterton made us see that romance lies, not in flitting, out of boredom, from one amorous adventure to another, but in experiencing, and returning, a life-long fidelity.

—*LIT,* 165–66

The fertility of his genius seemed inexhaustible.

—*LIT,* 166

Will Chesterton be remembered . . . ? That he himself should be speedily forgotten, is the prayer of every true prophet. He sees the world at fault, and fulminates accordingly; he would be only too glad that soon after his death . . . the world should have so thoroughly corrected its faults as to make the fulminations seem unnecessary. . . . There is more danger that he should be forgotten for the opposite reasons. It may be that the tendencies against which he fought, mass-production, industrial slavery, sentimental evasion of moral principles, senseless curtailment of human liberties, and so on, will come to be more and more with us, till the world finds it incredible that such protests as his were ever made.

—*LIT,* 168–69

Chesterton simply cannot be placed; he has no characteristic medium, but can make himself at home in any form of literary art, without obeying the rules of any.

—*LIT,* 193

He will most certainly be remembered as a prophet in an age of false prophets.

—*OCC*, 402

One of the very greatest men of his time. If posterity neglects him, it will pronounce judgment not upon him, but upon itself.

—*OCC*, 402

There is a legend told of his absent-mindedness that he once telegraphed home the words, "Am in Liverpool; where ought I to be?" And it took him fourteen years after the publication of his book *Orthodoxy* to find out that he ought to be in Rome.

—*OCC*, 403

The most important thing about Chesterton, he would have been the first to say it, the most distinctive quality in Chesterton was a quality which he shared with some three hundred million of his fellow men. He was a Catholic.

—*OCC*, 403

The most salient quality, I think, of his writing is this gift of illuminating the ordinary, of finding in something trivial a type of the eternal.

—*OCC*, 404

If every other line he wrote should disappear from circulation, Catholic posterity would still owe him an imperishable debt of gratitude, so long as a copy of *The Everlasting Man* enriched its libraries.

—*OCC*, 405

Chestertonians

If a man proclaims himself a Marxian, he has given you a line on his political and economic beliefs; a Wesleyan, he has named his theological creed; a Freudian, you know something of his approach to the problems of the unconscious. If he should call himself a Chestertonian, you would see his whole attitude mapped out; it would include all the values of life.

—LIT, 155

Chesterton's Father Brown

[It is] because the Father Brown stories are so good merely as detective stories, that it is possible to overlook the moral in most of them in your appreciation of their literary excellence—you are tempted, sometimes, to skip over the moral in your impatience to reach the explanation of the mystery.

—LIT, 167

It happened one day (I am told) that Chesterton had no literary work on hand—it seems a strange thing to imagine—and wandered into the office of my literary agent—who was also his—to know if there was any publisher wanting anything done. The reply was "Nothing in your line, I am afraid, Mr. Chesterton; in fact the only thing we have heard of lately is the *Saturday Evening Post* wanting some detective stories." To which he replied, "Oh, well, I don't know," and, sitting down there and then in the office, wrote the first of the Father Brown stories.

—LIT, 193

Children

Our Lord warns us that we cannot enter the kingdom of heaven except as children. What is the use of encouraging children to grow older, if the grand lesson of life is, after all, to learn to be as young as they?

—UAS, 411

Chivalry

All the modern nations . . . had the Church for their nursing-mother; they borrowed from her the first rudiments of their culture. It was, for example, so the historians tell us, the devotion to our blessed Lady which first produced that feeling of respect for womanhood which we call, in Christian Europe, by the name of chivalry.

—OCC, 213

Christian Hope

The Christian virtue of hope has nothing whatever to do with the world's future. As it was preached by the first apostles, it meant nothing more or less than a confidence on the part of the Christian that he or she would attain happiness in a future life. The world about them was perishable, and doomed to perish—perhaps in a very short time. . . . Again and again you find religious revivals accompanied by a belief in the impending dissolution of the world order. What does it matter, then, to us Christians, if we find the children of the world, like the fools they are, playing with fire? Let them destroy or devastate the planet; we, the elect, we, the remnant, see only a liberation from the weariness of this mundane existence, where they see calamity. Our hope lies, not in this world, but in the next; if it is true that the portents of our time give promise of a general conflagration, so much the better. It is doubtful if a world that has forgotten God, as ours has, can deserve or even desire a better fate. We always told them that their dream of a wiser and happier age was doomed to disappointment; now, perhaps, they will see that they were right.

—*GOD*, 117–18

Christianities

We Catholics . . . are apt to grow exasperated at the continued existence of other religious bodies, and to ask God why he allows people to go on believing in these half-truths, to the dishonour of the Catholic Church. We forget that God, in his providence, may permit these other religious bodies to exist, and even to flourish; for the reason, if for no other, that their existence is in some sort a protection to the Catholic Church, in days when the atheist and the materialist are making such determined attacks upon every form of organized religion.

—*OCC*, 176

Christianities (Post-Reformation)

The number of their adherents is steadily diminishing, and even those who do profess to adhere to them are more and more abandoning belief in the Bible, belief in revelation, belief in the sacraments, belief in a world of rewards and punishments hereafter. And it is not only their beliefs but their moral standards that are disappearing. Especially the sanctity of marriage is being profaned.

—*OCC*, 41

It is becoming a clear issue in our day, the [Catholic] Church or nothing.

—*OCC*, 41–42

Christianity

When you compare Christianity with Confucianism, you are comparing two systems of personal morality. When you compare Christianity with Mahomedanism, you are comparing two forms of fighting enthusiasm. When you compare Christianity with Buddhism, you are comparing two streams of mystical tendency. And, unconsciously, you have recognized that Christianity is something greater than the other three; because each of those others corresponds to one particular need, one particular mood.

—*HS*, 106

Christian thought, if you will look deep enough, is always turning out to be the *via media* between two opposing forms of error.

—*HS*, 219

A religion which has its roots so deep and its *rapports* so wide necessarily forms in the mind which lives by it an attitude, not merely to the next world but to this, traditions about the State and society, about marriage and the family, about the values of life, about the relative importance of various duties in life, and so on; these traditions would hold their own even if they were not reinforced, as at certain points they are reinforced, by the solemn judgment of the Church herself.

—*OCC*, 216

Not all the sophistries of Gibbon and his followers can blind the eye of the historian to the brute fact that the advent of Christianity is an epoch in the story of our planet; that, even if our faith be a dream, it is a dream that has been more profound in its influence than all the waking thoughts of the human imagination.

—*PAS*, 90

Christianity made easy is by no means Christianity made simple.

—SLS, 14

It began as a religion of slaves; it has destroyed slavery. It was thrown to the lions in the amphitheatre; it has abolished the amphitheatre. Absolute monarchy, like a flustered giant, laboured to crush it only till yesterday; it has outlived absolute monarchy. . . . Its vitality is inexhaustible . . . the world has not felt the full strength of it as yet . . . it still conquers men's hearts; you have only mistaken the morning mists for the chill of sunset. Look about you; it is the dawn.

—UAS, 361

The secret of Christianity is that there are no half-shares in it; you have to take it absolutely, and with all its consequences; you can't stop halfway, and say: "Look here, what exactly am I letting myself in for?" You cannot satisfy the claims of the Church with the cold homage of an intellectual assent, or with the distant bestowal on it of your distinguished patronage.

—UAS, 489

Christianity (Modern)

. . . [M]odern Christianity, a type which excels in organization, which loves nothing so much as committees and mass meetings. There is a spirit going abroad among many such people, which somehow makes out that it will be time enough to think about heaven when we get there. . . . To which I would reply, that on this showing there would be every excuse for saying, "It will be time enough to think about hell when we get there."

—UAS, 478

Christians

There is nothing more jealously watched or more bitterly criticized today by people who criticize religion than the behaviour of professed Christians. Fifty years ago, people did not pay very much attention to what we did; today, when the Catholic Church is the only considerable religious body that dares to claim an increasing and not a diminishing membership, we have a heavier responsibility.

—PAS, 99

From the first, Christians must learn what it means to be unpopular.

—PAS, 195

Are Christians, then, in general the victims of credulity, people who will believe anything? Or are they people of normally critical instincts, who, from a sentimental prejudice, make a single departure from their principles by consenting to believe in Jesus Christ? That is how some of our neighbours think of us; it seems natural to them when Easter Day falls on All Fools' Day. But we do not admit the imputation, in either form.

—PAS, 403

Christians (Ill-Rooted)

The sudden glare of the risen sun withers the ill-rooted stalks of wheat all in a moment; so the ill-rooted Christian is taken off his guard by the sudden incidence of persecution (Matt. xiii. 21). He will be taken off his guard like that, when he finds that to be a Christian is to be hated of all men (Matt. xxiv. 10); 'Oh, come', he will say, 'I never bargained for this; I never realized I was letting myself in for this!' He is thrown off his balance, by a scandal which is half Pharisaical; is he not secretly relieved to have an excuse for deserting the narrow way? Most of us have known converts who were scandalized like that, when they found that being a Catholic was not making an easy choice, and fell away, almost welcoming the opportunity.

— TOT, 70–71

Christian Science

I would say of the Christian Scientists that, if their results are really genuine, then it shows that will-power can do more in the way of interference with matter than we thought it could; just as, according to some stories one hears, it can enable men to stick knives into themselves without bleeding, or walk on hot iron without being scorched.

—UAS, 50

Christian Science and Spiritualism

The more these cults—the latter especially—succeed in winning ground, the less will be their strictly religious appeal. If miracles of healing became as common as the Christian Scientist would wish . . . we should take them for granted instead of getting excited about them. If the companionship of the dead became as familiar to us as the companionship of the living, the mystery would vanish, and all the element of faith which the system still demands. . . . In either case, the fruits of victory would disappear in the victor's hands; it is only because either case is still unproved that they continue to exercise fascination.

—CAL, 213

There are three facts in man's life which a complete religion offers to put in their right perspective—the problem of suffering, the fear of death, and the sense of sin. Christian Science has specialized on the first, Spiritualism on the second; both alike, as it seems to me, have neglected the urgency of the third. To the Christian Scientist, I understand, sin is an illusion like all other forms of evil, and our aim must be to boycott it by blinding ourselves to its existence— not an easy demand to make of ordinary people. The Spiritualist has overcome his fear of whatever terrors were supposed to lie beyond the grave; and, while he receives admirable moral advice, doubtless, from his familiars, is not enlightened by any theology of sin or of its consequences.

—CAL, 212

Christmas

A return to our origins.

—PAS, 354

The child who was born at Bethlehem had, for nine months, been carried in the womb at Nazareth, just like any other child; this is our guarantee that, although God, he was yet truly man. God did not deceive us by taking on the mere appearance of humanity . . . he *became* man; that was the leverage, if we may put it in very crude terms, through which the work of our redemption was effected. And, very curiously, this is one of the lessons which the Church found it particularly hard to teach. The early heretics were not people who denied our Lord's Godhead . . . they were people who denied his manhood.

—PAS, 355

Christus Rex (Feast of)

The claim of Christ comes first, before the claims of party, before the claims of nationality. *Pax Christi in regno Christi*; peace and justice were duties which man owed to God more elementary than any duties to his fellow men. All that, before the conflict between the Church and Fascism, before the revolution in Spain, before the name of Hitler had ever been set up in the type-room of a foreign newspaper. The institution of this feast was not a gesture of clericalism against anticlericalism, still less a gesture of authoritarianism against democracy. It was a gesture of Christian truth against a world which was on the point of going mad with political propaganda.

—PAS, 458

The Church

In ordinary circumstances, although it has never ceased to preserve the tradition of doctrine and of moral theory which (we believe) was handed down from the Apostles, it has only succeeded partially and with great difficulty in combating the bad traditions of its own more worldly supporters. . . . We are going to see the same struggle over birth control.

—DIF, 24

Truth is Truth, and has a right to be told; and even if I felt confident that a man was being saved outside the Church by following his lights faithfully, even if an angel from heaven revealed it to me, I should still want him to be enlightened with the fullness of the Catholic revelation, and should not feel justified in neglecting any opportunity for convincing him.

—DIF, 199

There is far more temptation not to believe in God than not to believe in the Church. For, as St. Thomas admitted, you have the whole fact of evil in Creation apparently against you, when you assert that God exists. . . . Whereas

48

the arguments against the Church always seem to me scraped together; they are like the thousand and one holes which a disgruntled man will find to pick in the character of a man or an institution he has quarrelled with.

—DIF, 230–31

Those who will take up the argument after me, my successors, will not be ashamed of me, nor I of them; that is the best of belonging to an impenitent Church.

—DIF, 241

The denial of an institutional Church leads, if it is pressed by ardent thinkers, to a denial of all validity in human institutions.

—EN, 122

More than all the other Christianities, the Catholic Church is institutional. Her enemies too easily conclude that she is thereby incapacitated from all spiritual initiative, David in Saul's armour; history makes short work of the conclusion.

—EN, 590

Christians who belong to other denominations don't even claim that their denomination is *the* Church. Church unity is something ... which will, it is to be hoped, come into existence again later on; it doesn't exist here and now. Anybody who has reached the point of looking round to find a single, visible fellowship of human beings which claims to be the one Church of Christ, has got to become a Catholic or give up his search in despair.

—HS, 117

When we say, then, that the teaching of the Church is the teaching of Christ, we mean two things. In the first place, that the substance of what we assert comes down to us, by continuous tradition, from his own teaching given to his apostles. In the second place that the formulae in which our belief is enshrined are the only true interpretation of his meaning, guaranteed to us by his promise that his Holy Spirit would guide the Church into all truth.

—ISG, 128

It is a human weakness of ours to be always crying out for complete novelty, an entire disseverance from our past. Our old traditions have become so dusty with neglect . . . that we are for casting them on the scrap-heap and forgetting that they ever existed. The Church conserves; she bears traces still of the Jewish atmosphere . . . traces, too, of the old heathen civilization which she conquered. And in her own history it is the same; nothing is altogether forgotten; every age of Christianity recalls the lineaments of an earlier time.

—OCC, 48

That is the secret of the modern world's antipathy towards . . . the Catholic Church in particular. They hate it not because it is something arrogant, not because it is something uncomfortable, not because it is something foreign, but because it is something out of date. They know that it will always bring new things and old out of its treasure-house, will not consent to the modern worship of the modern. And they know that there is strength in this deeply rooted tradition which can yet absorb, as it has absorbed all through the ages, lessons that are new.

—OCC, 50

A hundred years back [critics] hoped to dispose of the Church by disposing of the Bible; now their tactics have grown more subtle. They hope to dispose of the Church by disposing of Aristotle. It has become the fashion to gird at us because our whole thought is built up round a philosophical system which was fifteen hundred years old when we assimilated it, and has now ceased to hold the speculative allegiance of mankind.

—OCC, 50

Ever old, ever young, she encourages her children to sow beside all waters.

—OCC, 76

Still doomed to death, and fated not to die—so wrote our Catholic poet of the faith he had embraced; and this has been, everywhere and at all times, its history . . . our faith, a thing rooted in the past, wrapped up with a great deal of venerable imagery, of forgotten ceremony, of exploded tradition; so that even those who hate it will sometimes speak of it in tones of hushed respect, as men speak of the dead. But the fact is that it is alive . . . in the midst of all this modern hurry and heedlessness of the past, all this frantic worship of tomorrow.

—OCC, 134

The whole story of the Church is one which imitates the story of her divine Master; she dies, and she rises again. She was buried in the catacombs; she rose again with Constantine. She died in the Dark Ages; she rose again with Charlemagne. She died with the Renaissance; she rose again with the saints of the Counter-Reformation. You cannot kill the Catholic Church.

—OCC, 164–65

There must be something about the Catholic Church, whether it be creditable or discreditable, which will account for the way in which it is singled out by politicians sometimes for repression, and always for distrust.

—OCC, 215

It may be rent by a thousand discords, but its supernatural unity goes on undiminished.

—OCC, 231

Those who accept relief from it escape the sense of inferiority which hurts a man when he takes money from an individual; they escape, at the same time, that sense of pauperism which disgusts men with the more mechanical forms of organized relief. It is public, without being impersonal; it is charitable, without the detestable suspicion of patronage.

—OCC, 234

The Catholic Church is not merely a resting-place for this temperament or that. It is the resting-place of all minds, learned as well as simple, critical as well as enthusiastic; it has a welcome and a home for all.

—OCC, 239

The Catholic Church is the home of liberty, of Christ's followers who have freely received, and freely give.

—OCC, 281

The Church, militant on earth or triumphant in heaven, it is all one; and you and I are part of its organization, contribute, each of us, to the unity of the whole. We are not isolated units, like pebbles scattered on a beach; we are living stones, each of us occupying an appointed place in the divine scheme of architecture.

—OCC, 292

From generation to generation the torch has been handed on ... the Catholic Church doesn't hold together automatically on some merely mechanical principle. It depends from one generation to the next on a conspiracy of human wills. Our neighbours are so ready to believe that it is otherwise; that Catholics remain Catholics merely by force of habit; because they are too stupid to think of doing anything else; that to be a Catholic involves no strain, no effort of the mind, no combat with temptation.

—OCC, 360

If you come across people who have been priming themselves with Protestant theology ... it will not be long before you find somebody making the statement, that our Lord when he was on earth had no intention of founding a Church. If our Lord *did* mean to found a Church, then it is nonsense to imagine that he expected, or allowed his disciples to expect, that the world was coming to an end as soon as he died. And as a matter of fact there is plenty of evidence in the Gospels which shows that he did mean to found a Church ... evidence which is afforded by the parables, if you take the trouble to interpret them. The Sadducee of today, like the Pharisee of our Lord's time, goes wrong because he skims lightly over the parables ... without penetrating the theological mysteries which underlie them.

—PAS, 77

So in the Church, God's chosen seed-plot, the nursery of all sanctity, evil can strike deep roots in human souls, be their position in the Church never so exalted; can cling there with a desperate obstinacy, and can flaunt itself in such

52

a way that the careless onlooker will see in the Church nothing but a tangled mass of foul growths. Be shocked, be grieved, be indignant at scandals in the Church, but if you are a disciple of our Lord's parables do not be surprised at it. The worst of it has been foretold.

—*PAS*, 95

The whole controversy about the true Church is not whether it is the Roman Catholic Church or the Greek Church or the Anglican Church or some other definite religious body. The real controversy is this: Is the true Church of Christ a visible or an invisible institution? Ninety per cent of the people who reject the Catholic Church reject it, not because they really believe in some other visible Church, but because they do not believe in a visible Church at all.

—*PAS*, 97

The Catholic Church, again and again in her history, has undergone persecution or incurred angry criticism for precisely the same reason. She alone, in a world which had lost its sense of truth and contented itself with shams in which it half believed, asserted the claims of an absolute, because a revealed truth. And the world's reply has been to call her a deceiver. In the last days of paganism, when the old heathen gods had lost all their prestige, and their altars still smoked only in deference to a historic sentiment or a political convention, Christians were found asserting that there was one God.

—*PAS*, 182–83

She has been constantly assailed by her enemies either within or without. After the pagan persecutions, the heresies; after the heresies the barbarian inroads ... after the Mahomedans ... the great apostasy of the sixteenth century, then the horrors of the French revolution. Again and again the Church, like the apostles ... has been tempted to cry out in despair, "Master, doth it not concern thee that we perish?" And still, in answer to such doubts, the same reproof comes from him, "Why are you fearful, O ye of little faith?"

... For nineteen centuries men have been trying to repress the Catholic Church, and she emerges from the persecution chastised but not killed.

—*PAS*, 196

† Nowadays, & for quite a time, we have had "the world church" plugged heavily; but the idea is entirely "nebulous & nonsensical; it commits one to no definite beliefs or allegiances, & is just theological & social wind. (1997)

Nowadays, men tell us in a half-pitying, half-contemptuous tone that we belong to a dying religion! Let us accept the omen . . . we are, we always have been, a dying religion. From the first, we went underground in the catacombs; again and again we have been forced to our knees, fought a losing battle all down the centuries; do they think it is any news to us that the world is our enemy; persecutes us as it persecuted our Master? Today as yesterday, she is content to herald his death until he comes.

—PAS, 269

It is the first business of the Church to safeguard a deposit of revealed truth handed down to her, for all time, by a divine Founder; let her prove false to that trust, and the Church unchurches herself. Accordingly, our instinct as Catholics is conservative; the danger is always that we shall take our stand against new departures merely because they are new departures, and it is not difficult for our critics to represent us, at every turn, as worshippers of the past, enemies of all liberty and of all enlightenment . . . things are not as simple as that. Inside the Church as well as out of it, with larger issues at stake, and therefore with more anxious sense of responsibility, the question is discussed, "Is it wiser to go forward, or to protect what we have?"

—PAS, 431

It is not the faults, but the virtues of the Christian Church which make it unpopular.

—SLS, 3

Every Catholic knows that his Church is a splendidly happy-go-lucky affair— often haphazard, with sometimes internal quarrels—and that it would not hold together for ten years if there were not supernatural life and unity in this Divine Church.

—UAS, 379

The hallmark of historic Christianity. Wherever she goes, the world still hates the Church of Rome.

—UAS, 463

Church (Parish)

It is the expression, in architectural terms, of the parish at prayer. It sums up our history for us; we can look round us, and think of all the souls which have been nourished, generation after generation, at the same communion rails, all the stories of guilt which have been whispered and have died away at the same confessionals, all the new recruits in Christ's army who have been regenerated at the same font. We can remember, in Christ, our fellow worshippers who knelt here at our side, and are now separated from us in body, though still united to us with the same links of prayer. It is a kind of sacrament of the parish life.

—*OCC*, 315

The Church (Teachings of)

It is just these rules and regulations [for] which people outside the Church envy us. The measure of what they covet is the measure of what we would dare to throw away.

—*UAS*, 308

The Church and Politics

The Church is sometimes criticized for her want of courage, because she does not seek a direct issue with the tyrannical rulers of the modern age; force a conflict with them by forbidding their Catholic subjects to take any part as citizens in states so misgoverned. Curiously, another charge is often launched against the Church, which is exactly the opposite; and it is often launched by the same people. That charge is, that the Church is always interfering in secular matters which are beyond her province.

—*PAS*, 374

She believes that she has inherited from her divine Master a commission to act as the teacher and guardian of a moral order; she is a city set on a hill, and her light must not be hidden under a bushel. She could purchase for herself an inglorious peace by shutting herself up in the sacristy; but that is not how she interprets her commission. Nor is it only that she could purchase peace for herself; she could, humanly speaking, prevent many blasphemies and even formal apostasies, if she would sit quiet and let the politicians have their own way.

—PAS, 375

Christendom has before now taken up arms in its own defence; or even in a pathetic attempt to recover the Holy Places. Christian princes, before now, have tried to spread the faith at the point of the sword, always, or nearly always, with disastrous results for religion. But the substantial victories of the Church have lain, always, in the sphere of the human conscience. Christ has reigned, not in the councils of nations, but in men's hearts.

—PAS, 456

Church and State

Everywhere, even nowadays, in a hundred different forms, the old trouble between Church and State continues to crop up. So much so that Protestants loudly say, and we Catholics are sometimes tempted to think, that there must be something wrong with a Church which always seems to prove a storm-centre of political debate, even where it has no longer any temporalities to defend.

—OCC, 214–15

"Why cannot you Catholics leave politics alone?"—that is the cry which greets us everywhere, and sometimes wearies us. . . . Now, I think it is very often a fair answer to that question to say that the Church is quite prepared to leave politics alone when politics will be content to leave the Church alone.

—OCC, 215

Wherever you get a large body of Catholic citizens, especially when they have freedom for the interchange of ideas and opportunities for corporate action, they will necessarily form a kind of clique within the State, holding to, and defending, their own philosophy of life, which is a universal philosophy of life, against those particular fads and fashions which please that particular country at the particular period in history.

—OCC, 215

So you see in the United States the Catholic culture opposed, on the whole, to the Prohibition movement, a modern fad and a local one. . . . In Germany you will find it on the whole opposed to that militant nationalism which endangers the peace of Europe. . . . Very often, statesmen find this Catholic influence useful to them, as a kind of pendulum which redresses the eccentricities of the political machine, which stands for law and order and commonsense. But where a whole people is stampeded by some new fashion of thought, it cries out against this influence as something sinister, hostile, anti-social; Catholics cannot be good citizens, must be taking their orders from abroad, if they do not fall in with the catchwords which the fashion of a moment has made dominant.

−*OCC*, 216–17

It is extraordinary how people outside the Church, and even unreflecting people inside the Church, get that point wrong. They imagine that because the authority of the Pope is higher than the authority of a king—which it clearly is, because it belongs to the supernatural, not merely to the natural order—therefore the Pope claims to control the activities of all earthly rulers.

−*PAS*, 455

People's minds have got so accustomed to the idea of churches which are purely national in their outlook, that they cannot conceive the idea of a supra-national Church which is not for ever interfering in politics. When we say that, there's no need to disguise the fact that conflicts do often arise between the Catholic and the civil authorities in a country, simply because in practice the delimitation between the secular and the spiritual spheres is so hard to achieve perfectly.

−*PAS*, 455

The struggle between Church and State is not yet dead. Already people are expecting the Church to alter her laws of kindred and affinity to match the State's laws. . . . The sword will pierce our hearts too—not the bared sword of forcible oppression, but the more deadly weapons of contempt, criticism, ridicule, protest, oblivion. Mutilated creeds, half-hearted devotions, up-to-date formularies, will be pressed upon our acceptance. . . . When the crisis comes . . . we shall need all the prayers [and] self-discipline of St. Thomas . . . to see that the spiritual crown . . . of inner meekness and humility is not taken away from us.

−*UAS*, 515–16

The Church as Institution

[The apostles] were not, then, merely witnesses whom he must always have about him, they were something more important than that; the nucleus round which his Church was to grow. And so it is to them he speaks in words such as he never uses in his public discourses: "As the Father hath sent me, I also send you . . . whose soever sins you remit, they are remitted unto them, and whose soever sins you retain, they are retained"; and to St Peter above all he gives the privilege of immovable faith, and the power to bind and to loose. You see, then, that our Lord from the first meant his Church to centre round a hierarchy; took more trouble, you may say, about forming the character and confirming the faith of the Church's future rulers than about baptizing people or making converts; indeed, when he ascended into heaven, the Church he left behind him was only a Church of 120 souls. But he had the nucleus; he had the *cadre* of his army, the rank and file could wait. And that means, clearly, that it was his intention to leave behind him an institution with a visible membership, with rules, with officials, in a word, an organized Church.

—*ISG*, 79

Churches

A church in alliance with the world has unchurched itself.

—*EN*, 590

Church of England

[The Church of England] is . . . but a sort of compound of lights and green stoles and bad brass and the Church of England Men's Society, and the Holy Eucharist at eight and Matins at eleven, and confession if you happen to feel like it, and doctrine which forgets Paul, and discipline which defies Peter, and devotion which has never heard of Mary. That is, dear brethren, the official religion of the present Church of England.

—*UAS*, 457

How long will it be before the Church of England ceases to affirm the sanctity of the marriage tie?

—*UAS*, 459

I prophesy this: if the Church of England cannot find, within the next fifty years, some authority for itself which can claim, as a matter of divine right, and not of administrative convenience, to interpret the Scriptures and expel heresy from its borders, then, humanly speaking, in fifty years' time it will be a Church to which you and I will find it impossible to belong.

—UAS, 459

Church of the Future

The all-embracing Church of the future should find room, not only for the Mahommedans and Buddhists, but also for the atheists. I pointed out that we Christians had only one quarrel, after all, to patch up with the atheists, namely, as to whether God existed or not; and I concluded, as far as I remember, that in some future age we should all come to recognize a God "who exists, yet does not exist, causes sin, yet hates it, hates it, yet does not punish it, and promises us in heaven a happiness which we shall not have any consciousness to enjoy". I only wanted to point out to some of my fellow-Christians how close their tolerance was leading them to a position of pure agnosticism.

—BCM, 39–40

Church Services

What an extraordinary thing it is that nobody minds waiting five minutes for a train, but if you wait five minutes in church for a service to start it always feels like hours.

—OCC, 18

Church Tradition

We can only be certain about any of our Lord's promises or statements, we can only be certain that there is a Heaven or a way of getting there, if we believe that his teaching has been transmitted to us by means of a continuous tradition; which tradition is in the keeping of an institution; which institution (like all other institutions) must have power to expel refractory members, and reject attempts to tamper with its own vital principles. We don't think that Catholics are more likely to be right about religious truths because they "conform most closely to God's will" in general. We know that they are the only people who can possibly be right about religious truths, because they are the only people who have a theory to justify the claim that their own doctrines correspond with the teaching given by our Lord to his Apostles.

—*OR*, 130–31

Civilization

Civilization is not a gospel which has to be preached, it is an influence which pervades, a leaven which automatically overcomes.

—*OTO*, 124

Communion

I wonder, is that why some of us are so frightened of holy communion, because we still cling so to the world of sense? It is certain that Catholics are most apt to neglect communion just when they most need it; in the spring-time of youth, when . . . ambition dominates us. Why is that, unless that we are more wedded, when we are young, to the desires that perish? I wonder, is that why so many of us who go often to communion find . . . that we are still as full of bad habits as we were ten or fifteen years ago, that our lives . . . compare unfavourably with the lives of others, who have not our opportunities for going to communion frequently? Is it perhaps because, all the time, we are shrinking from the act of confidence which would throw the whole burden of our lives on our Lord?

—*PAS*, 206

A saintly Pope, the tenth Pius, was filled with the spirit of his Master, and said, like his Master, "I am moved with pity for the multitude." For the multitude . . . who fall short, all the time, of the Christian ideal. We were hungry for spiritual nourishment in a desert world, a world that had largely forgotten God, fallen in love with the pitiable illusion of human progress, and St Pius taught us that frequent and daily communion was not to be thought of as a rare privilege of the cloister . . . for a life of uninterrupted devotion in God's service. It was to be our talisman against every-day temptations, our salve for every-day shortcomings.

—*PAS*, 289

Congregations

Ideally the parish priest and his congregation form a single unit of Christendom
.... The parish priest is the spiritual father, who regenerates you at the
font; ... who feeds you; he corrects, where it is needed, your faults. And you
are brothers and sisters, who meet, week by week, at a common table, bound
together at once by human neighbourliness and by a common faith. You are
meant to find your salvation not as lonely individuals, ... but as members of a
single organism, helping one another, encouraging one another, each making
his or her contribution to the life of the whole.

—OCC, 368

Conscience

Conscience remains superior to all direction, to all controls. Precisely when
you extort submission from a man by bullying and browbeating him, you
have failed to secure your object, because there was no free consent. Conscience is free.

—OCC, 279

Conscience of Humanity

Don't let us fall into the error of saying that I don't obey my conscience, but
the general conscience of humanity. That is what these modern people are
always trying to do; I got a letter only the other day from somebody who
wanted me to sign a letter protesting against the persecution of the Jews
"before the conscience of civilization." But civilization is an abstraction, and it
hasn't got a conscience. What they mean is, a collection of consciences
belonging to a collection of civilized people; just as when they talk about the
universal mind they only mean a collection of individual minds.

—ISG, 17

Contemplatives

The world . . . does not understand the love that waits, any more the love that
weeps.

—UAS, 397

The contemplative has reserves of silent strength which the world never dreams of.

— UAS, 397

Contemplatives (Paradox of)

The closer a soul draws to [God], the more conscious it becomes of the infinite distance which separates itself from him; itself, a creature, itself, a sinner.

— UAS, 395

Conversion

Over . . . death-bed conversions, the world sees fit to make merry, and to reflect what a pleasant affair the Catholic religion must be. Do as you like all your life, indulge your passions as you will, and then . . . seventeen words mumbled by a priest, and all is well; you are safe for eternity. Well, these labourers of the eleventh hour have a patron, the good thief who was crucified beside our Lord.

— PAS, 143

Essentially, all conversion is one. The same thing happens when a Protestant receives the gift of faith as happens when a drunkard at a parish mission gets the grace to live sober; as happens in a retreat, when some soul, after many hesitations, decides to give itself up more completely to God—perhaps in the life of the cloister. It is God's will taking over, and man's will saying "Carry on."

— OCC, 242

Converts

Here is a free man. It is not enough that we, we Catholics, should hold out hands to welcome him. He should claim the applause of millions who do not share our faith, yet love the truth. He has risen to the stature of a free man.

— OCC, 280

There is a story of a convert in Newcastle who was asked why he became a Catholic, and he said he tried all the other places of worship, and everywhere they thrust a hymn-book into his hand, and stood at the door asking him to come again—except the Catholic church, where nobody took any notice of you at all.

—OR, 122

Country Houses

The vacuity of a country house early in the morning, who does not know it? Except those fortunate people who are always, and by instinct, late for breakfast.

—LIT, 90

Creating

You and I never create—that is to say, we never create out of nothing.

—UAS, 362

The Creation

It is not true that the emergence of organic from inorganic matter is the test case by which Christian theology seeks to prove the intervention of a Creator; not true, therefore, that if (in some inconceivable way) the distinction between organic and inorganic matter could be abolished, the argument for a Creator would fall to the ground; not true that, if some scientist were to succeed in producing synthetic life, he would be usurping something which must necessarily be regarded as a Divine privilege. It is notorious that, throughout the Middle Ages, spontaneous generation continued to be regarded as a normal scientific view. It is difficult, therefore, to imagine how any formula by which life should emerge as the result of some chemical process could bring distress to Christian consciences.

—BCM, 266

I always find it so hard to imagine how people can look at the order of creation around them and content their minds with the supposition that it got there by chance. Nothing but dead matter to start with, and then mysteriously

63

arising amidst that dead matter living things, with the power of organic growth; and then amidst those living things, mysteriously again, conscious things, capable of feeling and of moving from place to place; and then amidst those conscious things, still more mysteriously, a self-conscious being.... What do they make of it all, the materialists?

—UAS, 6–7

Crisis

An atmosphere of crisis takes people different ways. Some get so wrapped up in their work that they never look beyond the edge of their own cabbage-patch. Others think in continents, and are depressed, nowadays, by the exercise; what is the use of doing anything, when everything is going from bad to worse? The Christian ought to rise above both those temptations. His daily work, his common human duties, are a charge entrusted to him. He believes in the sacrament of the present moment; what might happen, what is likely to happen, he leaves in the hands of God.

—LIG, 122

Criticism

If there is anything pleasant in criticism, it is finding out what we aren't meant to find out. It is the method by which we treat as significant what the author did not mean to be significant, by which we single out as essential what the author regarded as incidental. Thus, if one brings out a book on turnips, the modern scholar tries to discover from it whether the author was on good terms with his wife; if a poet writes on buttercups, every word he says may be used as evidence against him at an inquest of his views on a future existence. On this fascinating principle, we delight to extort economic evidence from Aristophanes, because Aristophanes knew nothing of economics: we try to extract cryptograms from Shakespeare, because we are inwardly certain that Shakespeare never put them there: we sift and winnow the Gospel of St. Luke, in order to produce a Synoptic problem, because St. Luke, poor man, never knew the Synoptic problem to exist.

—ESS, 145–46

Criticism does not love the unpredictable.

−*LDD,* 206

Critics

Our critics, in every kind of art, will only let us admire what is flung at us as a smudge, supposedly representing some impression in the artist's mind, all the better for being shapeless. To smell of the midnight oil damns you.

−*LIT,* 200

The Cross

The cross itself is a providentially appointed sign of contradiction, the very sign spoken of by Simeon in the temple. It cancels, it erases; bids us take no notice of what was there before, and start again. And that is symbolic of the fact that Christianity and the world are perpetually at cross-purposes.

−*LAY,* 79–80

The Crucifixion

Our conception of the sacrifice of the Cross gains, instead of losing, if we believe that the death was voluntary in the sense, not merely that he brought it on himself by opposition to the unfaithful shepherds of Israel, but that he might, up to the last moment, have saved himself: there was no point at which his sacrifice did not demand a continuous act of the will on his own part.

−*SLS,* 94–95

This historical tragedy does not merely represent for us, as other great tragedies may, the sins and the sorrows of the world. It is not a mere imaginary instance which illustrates their meaning. It does actually sum up, does actually contain within itself, all the sins and all the sorrows of the world. It does not merely illustrate the great injustices of the world, it contains them. Jesus Christ hanging upon his cross is the head of our redeemed humanity; and all the world's sins are his punishment, and all the world's sorrows are his crown.

−*UAS,* 381–82

Cultural Secularization

Has it made no difference, this tacit, public abandonment of the creed by which our grandfathers lived? The legal restraints which once safeguarded faithfulness in marriage have all gone. Decency itself is little sought after; how a man likes to behave is his own affair, as long as he doesn't interfere with the convenience of other people. And honesty—we have not said good-bye to honesty, but how much harder a business it seems to be, nowadays, deciding what is honest and what isn't!

$-OCC$, 311

D

Darwinism

Even Darwin did not really alter the status of orthodox theology, for if we had not, in the eighteenth century, realized that Man developed from an apparently soulless thing, the monkey, we all knew that every man develops from what appears to be an equally soulless thing, the baby.

—SLS, 8

Day of Judgment

I doubt if the modern theologian really regards this possibility as a possibility. Should it be realized, we should hear him ... attempting to delay the trumpet-message with the protest, "Wait a moment! Wait, till we have converted India and China. Wait, till the Labour Movement is more in touch with Christianity. Wait, till we have settled up our differences with Nonconformity: till we have brought Constantinople to our side, and Rome to her knees."

—SLS, 10

Death

I sometimes wonder whether it may not be true that everybody, at the moment of death, receives some kind of illumination. ... And it is conceivable that in some such interim God does speak to the soul; though it is only in the case of Saints and very good people that the illumination begins before the faculties have ceased to function. I am not suggesting that everybody there-

67

upon repents, which would do away with the possibility of eternal punishment; only that our judgments as to who is saved and who is lost may be much further out than we ordinarily assume.

—DIF, 208

Death means rest; rest from hard work, from acute pain, from all the regrets and solicitudes which haunt the mind. That moral is clear enough, even to the mind of a pagan who does not believe in a future life.

—LAY, 192

Every man born into this world lives in a condemned cell; the warrant for his death will be issued not at an hour of his own choosing.

—OCC, 141

Death has this to answer for—it disturbs our scale of values. Life is full of relationships so trivial, so undignified, that Death strikes a false note when it enters into them. Two lovers, for example, naturally think of the moment, and speak with pathos of the moment, when Death will part them. Nobody thinks of the moment when Death will part him from his dentist. It is a cruel, brutal thing when you see it shorn of all its paraphernalia of tragedy.

—OTO, 7

There are so many other things to be done in the world, so many echoes that deafen us, that we are apt to forget the first principle of our probation, which is this: that the most important moment of our lives, the moment around which all the rest of our life ought to be grouped as its centre and its climax, is the moment when we leave it.

—PAS, 117

The Deceased

Oughtn't we to think of our Christian dead as a great multitude surrounding us, like the lights of a city when you look across the valley at evening; some brighter, some paler, some nearer, some more distant, but all reflecting, each in its degree, the beauty and the majesty of God? Some will need our prayers more than others; some, more than others, will be able to bestow a blessing on us in return.

—OCC, 318–19

Strange, and perhaps humiliating, that our memories of the lately dead should be so much preoccupied with the little tricks of personality, the jokes, the prejudices, the poses of the living man we knew; that they should reach so little to the inner heart of him, to the secret springs of character and of motive which God alone sees, which alone God judges . . . we would like to distil, if we could, some essential fragrance from the character of the departed which should inform our gratitude for his friendship and inspire, a little, our own lives from his memory.

—OCC, 401

When we are thinking of dead friends, don't we usually find that all the faults we had to accuse them of vanish into the background . . . the defects of birth and upbringing; and the souls of the departed, lit up by that haze of gracious reminiscence, lose the shadows that stood out so boldly when we criticized them in life? . . . So we speak, vying with one another to make amends to the poor corpse for all the criticisms we have made in years past. And, meanwhile, that soul has stood on its trial, and is expiating, in purgatory, the stains of its conversation here.

—PAS, 466–67

Denial

There is a fresh temptation to worldliness which we have to face. . . . I mean the temptation to lie low about it as far as possible, run away from the subject of religion when it crops up in conversation, talk about the Church in a rather detached and dispassionate way, as if we only half belonged to it. I do not say there is anything positively sinful in that attitude; only, it is running away from the cross.

—PAS, 376

Descartes, René

The effect of Descartes upon philosophy, or rather on the estimation in which philosophy is held by the general public, has been fatal. The whole Idealist approach assumes that the human mind is an instrument you can be certain of, and that it does not really make much difference whether you can be certain of the external world or not; thought can go on indefinitely spinning its own web, like the spider with its own stomach for work-box, never acknowledging any debt to brute matter. But, . . . other philosophers arose who questioned the validity of these purely mental intuitions. The same hesitations about the reality of our sensible experience which convinced Berkeley that there must be a God from whom our ideas were borrowed, convinced Hume that you could have no certainty about anything at all.

—GOD, 28

To him, the idea of God was an idea self-luminous and therefore true; you did not have to prove the existence of God from the existence of the world around you; rather, you had to prove the existence of the world around you from the existence of God.

—HS, 12

Destiny

Man alone among the creatures has been dignified with a free will and a choice of destinies, that he might be God's fellow-artist, that he might co-operate with his Creator in moulding for himself a destiny which is eternal.

—UAS, 365

Detective Stories

It may be reasonably maintained that a detective story is meant to be read in bed, by way of courting sleep; it ought not to make us think. . . . If this is so, have we not good reason to complain of an author who smuggles into our minds, under the disguise of a police mystery, the very solicitudes he was under contract to banish?

—LIT, 177–78

Nature abhors a vacuum; and the supply of novels which were all character and no plot created a demand for novels which were all plot and no character. Hence the rise of the detective novel.

—*LIT,* 180

Many great men—it is notorious—read detective stories, though often behind locked doors, or under false jackets. They are afraid of their high-brow friends; for detective stories still do not rank as literature ... and if you meet a man who boasts that he does not think them interesting, you will nearly always find that he indulges in some lower form of compensation—probably he is a cross-word addict.

—*LIT,* 181

The Devil

It is so stupid of modern civilization to have given up believing in the devil ... he is the only explanation of it.

—*LDD,* 214

The Devil is an excellent tactician, and inspires us to unimagined flights of generalship when we ought to be thinking about something else.

—*OCC,* 219

It isn't true that there had to be a devil. According to Catholic theology, the devils were created good and were meant by God to be good; only he determined to create them as beings having a moral power of choice; and it is not possible, not conceivable, I mean, to give a person the power of choice without making it possible for him to choose wrong. God didn't create a "state of bad and good"; he created, ... a possibility of bad and good, by placing some of his creatures, whether angels or men doesn't matter, in a condition in which they could choose for themselves. There is a particular kind of thing, namely right-choosing, which God himself couldn't have put into the world he was creating without introducing the possibility of evil.

—*OR,* 21

71

Dignity

Half the trouble in the world comes from people standing on their own dignity.

— UAS, 363

Diplomacy

God forbid that relations between man and man should be modelled on those of rival peoples when they are at war. We have all come to accept it as a regrettable fact that policy in war-time is only a byproduct of strategy; and we grant the diplomatist the same latitude which is claimed by the general in the field, of concealing, and even misrepresenting, his designs. We should not care to do business with a man who had learned his sense of truthfulness in a Ministry of Propaganda. And there is in diplomacy, apart from the question of truth, an undertone of bullying, blackmailing and bargaining which might pass muster in big business, but would scarcely endear a man to his friends.

— GOD, 79

Divine Being

When God appeared to Moses, he revealed himself under the title I AM WHO AM; and theologians have read in those simple words the most profound truth about the divine Being—that there is no distinction of essence and existence, of attributes and personality, in him; his goodness, his wisdom, his power, his justice, are nothing other than himself.

— OCC, 89

Divine Providence

Divine Providence, instead of being an asset to Christian apologetics, is a heavy liability. We've got to believe in it, if we are going to make any sense of our religion at all;...neither Scripture nor common sense will allow us to doubt it. But the facts...seem to be against us. However many blessings we have to be thankful for, there is a great deal of evil all around us, physical and moral evil, and we are inclined to wonder why God, being

72

infinitely powerful, infinitely wise, and infinitely good, should have included so much evil in the scheme of things—or, for that matter, any evil at
all.

—OCC, 332

Divine Revelation

Truth is something homelier and friendlier than bare intellectual conviction.
Revealed truth does not merely claim the homage of our intellects, it satisfies
the aspirations of our hearts.

—OCC, 250

Divine Right

We have ceased to believe in the Divine Right of kings; but it is meaningless to
disbelieve in the Divine Right of God.

—SLS, 6

Doctrine

It doesn't do to say that heresy produces the development of doctrine, because
that annoys the theologians. But it is true to say that as a matter of history the
development of doctrine has been largely a reaction on the Church's part to
the attacks of heresy.

—HS, 139

The defined doctrines ... are guaranteed by a promise of Divine guidance;
whatever else is or is not true, these must be true. Therefore, you must resign
your conclusions, you must submit your reasoning processes to the refutation
of this higher certainty.

—SLS, 231

Dogma

An extraordinary superstition has grown up nowadays that a dogma is something which is forced down the throats of an unwilling public by an official caste which feels competent to instruct it; the Latin word *dogma*, you know, derived from the verb *doceo, I teach.* It need hardly be pointed out that this whole modern use of the word *dogma* is a misuse of it; that a dogma is exactly the opposite of what these people mean by it. It is not a Latin word at all; it comes from the Greek verb δοκεῖ, *it seems good,* and means, not something which one man tries to force down the throats of other men, but something on which a number of different people, coming to the question from different parts of the world and with different mental backgrounds, are all unanimously agreed.

— CAL, 15

More dogma is wanted, pulpitfuls of it.

— SLS, 218

Donatism

Men who are courting martyrdom do not lend themselves to gentle handling, and men who have an exaggerated cult for martyrs are not likely to underestimate, when the time comes to exchange stories of atrocities.

— EN, 57

What fixed the Donatist *ethos,* and distinguished it from that of Catholics, was in the last resort nothing else than an exaggerated veneration for martyrdom.

— EN, 60

Doubt

You and I have got all the apparatus in us for doubting every article of the Christian creed; faith is not a knife which cuts them out; it is an injection which neutralizes them. Many of us have bad times, perhaps when we wake up at four in the morning and can't go to sleep again, when the whole of religion *seems* absolutely unreal to us. And at such times we don't merely see the point of the atheist's line of argument, we feel the attraction of it.

—*HS,* 20

Drunkenness

It is proverbial, that drunkenness encourages speech on occasions, and in company, where a sober man would have kept his feelings to himself. But that is not to say that drunkenness is the sole cause of the feelings expressed; its effect is rather to translate feelings into speech. A man swears more when he is drunk, not because he is more annoyed, but because he cannot control the expression of his annoyance; makes love more freely, not because his sentiments of love are deeper, but because he has overcome the embarrassment which held him tongue-tied. And if he confesses his sins when he is drunk, it is not because he has more consciousness of sin, but because he has less shame about referring to it in public.

—*BCM,* 102–3

E

Ecumenism

All this talk about reunion assumes, necessarily, that the one Church which Christ founded on earth has, in process of time, been split into a set of fragments—the Easterns, the Anglicans, the Wesleyans, and so on. Each of these will have preserved some part of Christian truth, some more than others. To us Catholics such language is meaningless; we have not so learned Christ. For us, the Church is nothing less than his Temple, his Bride, his own Body; and the idea that it could, by any conceivable historical circumstances, be split into fragments, is a blasphemy. The reunion of the Churches is to us not merely impossible, it is unthinkable. You cannot reunite what has never been divided. For the Catholic Church to take part in a reunion of the Churches would be a . . . contradiction in terms.

—OCC, 197

Education (Age of)

It was, and is, an over-educated age that needs to sit at the feet of an under-educated saint.

—UAS, 411

Education (Catholic)

If *we* don't educate our children someone else will. In our day . . . someone else is the State; and the state we can be quite certain, will make a hash of it.

−*UAS*, 413

Education (Modern)

A sense of history, a sense of language—these are coming to be regarded as luxurious extras in the curriculum of education, hardly to be acquired in the intervals of that practical schooling which, before long, will qualify every citizen to mend his own wireless set.

−*GOD*, 19

Education produces people, in the mathematical sense; it just exaggerates the ideas they started with.

−*LDD*, 260

Education (Religious)

People always complain, young people specially, that they were not taught Christian doctrine at school. It would be more modest as well as more accurate to say that they did not learn Christian doctrine at school.

−*PAS*, 377

Efficiency

We are all coming to worship efficiency, instead of magnificence.

−*SLS*, 4

The Elect

The many who are called, then, constitute the Church, the thing called out; and the fact that many are called but few chosen means that the Church is something other than the whole body of the redeemed. The Ecclesia is one thing, the Elect are another; and it was the capital mistake of early Protestantism that it never realized that.

—PAS, 94

Enemies

The Church clings, obstinately, to the instinct which tells her that [our enemies], too, are somehow partakers of the altar; no Mass is complete unless they, too, are remembered. An empty place at table, yes, and an empty chair by the fireside, but not an empty place at the communion rail—that sacrament which unites the living unites too, somehow, the living with the dead.

—PAS, 211

England

No expense can be too heavy for producing a film, for putting on a revue, for hiring a football professional. We dance all night, and play tennis all day.... But is there not something suspicious about this feverish gaiety of ours ... this dreary cry for the unsexing of women.... Our expert critics, do they bid us believe that all is well with England? Is our gaiety real, or is it a smile painted on the face of a corpse?

—OCC, 11–12

The country of compromises.

—SLS, 217

A nation of busybodies.

—UAS, 317

In England prejudice dies harder than religion.

—UAS, 355

Englishmen

Englishmen on the whole do not tell lies. . . . I don't think they tell the truth. . . . A very difficult thing to do.

—DIF, 229

The late Canon Barry, I am told, used to maintain that "it takes a Frenchman or an Italian to commit a mortal sin"—his notion being that the Englishman is always in such a confused state of conscience as to be incapable of deliberately offending God.

—LDD, 66

English Religion and the Moderns

The ordinary Englishman's attitude towards religion is wonderfully vague, and his tolerance of other people's immoralities almost inexhaustible; but he has not given up, and shows no sign of giving up, the terminology and the outward symptoms of religious belief. This has set up, I think, a feeling of irritation in the prophets of the New Age; they are disgusted to find the corpse still twitching. And they are disgusted equally with the reaction in intelligent circles against the propaganda of unbelief; with scientists and philosophers who preach, amid the confusions of our modern thought, a return to earlier loyalties. It is this mood of exasperation which I find chiefly reflected in their writings; more than a century since Darwin, and still there are Prayer-book debates, and a Vatican City!

—BCM, 29

Enlightenment (Age of)

The age of enlightenment was also an age of fanaticisms.

—EN, 388

Enthusiasm (Religious)

Every enthusiasm tends to isolate some one Catholic doctrine, and to exaggerate its emphasis.

−*EN*, 409

Enthusiasts (Religious)

In the mind of the ordinary believing Christian, the two principles of reason and revelation are interlocked; a theologian will sort them out and delimit their spheres for you, but in everyday life there is an unconscious give-and-take which regulates your thought. . . . It is not so with the convert to enthusiasm. In his mind, a sudden *coup d'état* has dethroned the speculative intellect altogether. . . . You must not *think*; that would be to use the arm of flesh, and forsake your birthright.

−*EN*, 486

Eternity

It is eternity which matters, and time does not count.

−*OCC*, 87

The Eucharist

Our Lord used to preach even to his enemies. But even among the rough and tumble of the crowd who listened to him, what a lot of half-hearted disciples there must have been! Would he not have done better to gather round him a little nucleus of really faithful souls? But no, he had something for everybody. So it is in the Holy Eucharist; you would think it would have been jealously reserved for a handful of the very elect, a gift so holy. But no; it is for the rough and tumble of us as well.

−*LIG*, 71–72

This sacrament is by its very title, in its very origin, a sacrament of thanksgiving.

−*PAS*, 222

The Blessed Sacrament is the sacrament of unity; and when you receive it, it does not merely produce in you more charity towards your neighbour, more loyalty towards the Church, more unselfishness in your human attachments. It makes you more at unity with yourself.

—PAS, 238

Every communion is Christ going about to do good.

—PAS, 320

Eugenics

What you call Eugenics I call Dulogenics: it is the breeding of slaves. God made man in his own image, we are preparing to create the ideal man in ours. In our image, reflecting all our fads, all our prejudices, by predestination from his birth.

—SAF, 45

Eugenics and the State

Now, in every country where State-worship gets the upper hand, there is something peculiarly ominous about a conspiracy between the men of action and the men of science. There is the danger that they will start experimenting with human lives, labelling people unfit and disqualifying them from public life, breeding selectively, conditioning, as far as that is possible, the minds and the habits of the young. In plain words, it is slavery; we killed it in Germany, but we have not heard the last of it. And wherever it begins to flourish, there will be a temptation for the men of science to sell their souls.

—OCC, 265

Evangelicals

For the Evangelical (illogically, perhaps, but by habit) regards the Bible, not the inner light, as the ultimate source of theological certainty. But, in so far as he is true to type, he will reject the interpretations offered to him by scholars. He prefers to get down 'his' Bible and 'see what it says'; from the plain sense of it there is no appeal.

—EN, 586

At the heart of him, the Evangelical is always an experimentalist. He feels certain that something has happened to him, and he invites you to let it happen to you — that is, really, the whole of his message.

—EN, 587

That there should be a few people, close friends of God, who seem to live by instinct and by-pass calculation, is well enough; even the common run of us may experience, now and again, a flash of intuition which seemed akin to inspiration. But when a whole sect aspires to be spoon-fed with providential guidance, such as makes all deliberation, all effort of decision, henceforth unnecessary, there is ground for misgiving.

—EN, 587

Evangelism (Modern)

[Evangelism] does not believe in salvation of grace apart from works, and the damnation of all those who do not approve of its tenets. . . . it tends to accommodate itself to the convenience of the world.

—UAS, 463

Evolution

All mechanism yesterday, it was all evolution today. And evolution was a category under which you could rearrange every department of experience; civilization was evolving, . . . thought was evolving, religion was evolving, there was no limit to it. Instead of the endless wheels that used to turn in our heads when we could not get to sleep, nightmare figures succeeded; "dragons of the prime that tore each other in their slime", whose struggle to exist would last eternally; all our struggles were only the continuation of theirs. Instead of the dreary confidence that nothing ever changed, we had a dreary confidence that nothing ever remained the same; we were back at Heraclitus' difficulty; all was flux, and we were part of it.

—GOD, 31

Evolution and Theology

It is not true that Christian tradition was, till Darwin came, pledged to the notion of fixed types, as numerous at the beginning of the world as they are today. Anybody who will take the trouble to consult Dr Messenger's recent book on *Evolution and Theology* will find that some of the Fathers of the Church, noticeably St Augustine, anticipated our modern ideas in a remarkable way, though, of course, not from the angle of experimental research. The view that the body of man is developed from a common stock with the apes remains, on the one side, a theory which still lacks decisive confirmation; remains, on the other side, a theory which the Church has not condemned. It may be pointed out that the infusion of a soul into a creature which was merely animal by ancestry would in itself be no more surprising than the infusion of a soul into the human foetus.

—*BCM*, 265

Evolution, Theory of

People went about with long faces cursing Darwin and the other people for tracing man's ancestry, ... from some monkey or monkeys unknown. They minded that terribly; not so much, I think, because they were Christians as because in their heart of hearts they were good old solid Victorians, who thought that the human species ... was the highest kind of existence that could possibly be conceived. ... But if they'd looked in the Bible, instead of being so anxious to defend the accuracy of the Bible, they'd have found something much worse than that. The Bible says the Lord God formed man out of the slime of the earth. That's what we are, Lord Macaulay and all the rest of us, slime. ... We are animals, we are organisms, we are matter—slime of the earth.

—*GOD*, 13

Existence

We are impressed, as a rule, by the swift flight of time, by the transitoriness of human existence. How they outlive us, the works of our own hands; how they dwarf our human stature, the trees our grandfathers planted, the stones men piled on one another a couple of centuries back!

—*OCC*, 345–46

Experience

"Experience" for authority, a modern form of compensation . . . experience is
a precious poor light for anyone who is searching, as you are searching, for
religious truth. And what guidance it gives, for all I could ever see, brings you
straight up against the Catholic Church, whose doors you find still closed to
you.

—*DIF,* 237

Sic transit gloria mundi, "So passes the glory of this world." Man was born for
eternity, and every experience of his, when he comes to look at it afterwards,
is found to be unsatisfying, not simply because it was impermanent, but
because all the while it was imperfect.

—*PAS,* 275

Experts (Modern)

He does not make any sustained attack on religion; he dismisses it in a series of
contemptuous allusions, giving us to understand that he is too busy talking
about science to delay over such trifling matters. Meanwhile he contrives to
insinuate that religion and science are necessarily incompatible; that everything,
therefore, which he has said in praise of science is *ipso facto* a condemnation of
religion. He will belittle Christianity by forced contrasts; now dwelling on
the long "aeons" which elapsed between the protoplasm and the appearance of Moses, now showing how ignorant and brutish the Middle Ages were
by comparison with the civilization that dates from Darwin. He is the prophet
of a new age, and he has the public ear. He astounds with outpourings of
quaint scientific facts; he dazzles with glimpses of the incomprehensible. He
creates the *impression* that religion is of yesterday, science of today.

—*BCM,* 22–23

F

Fads

Solidity, permanence, authority . . . what is it people are looking for today? We are given pounds made of paper, and shillings made of tin, and that depreciation in our currency is only a symbol of the depreciation in the currency of ideas which our age is witnessing. Right and wrong, sin and virtue, decency, modesty—do such names as these retain the old meaning and the old recognition? We still use them, and we still mean them, but somehow we're not quite sure what we mean *by* them.

—UAS, 308

Fads (Intellectual)

There are fashions in human thought; mechanism was the keyword of the century before last, evolution of the century that has just gone, relativity of our own. Philosophy goes round in circles, now realism will be the dominant teaching, . . . there is no fixed point, we are always changing. And always when the recognition of God's existence becomes obscured in the public consciousness, thought turns back upon itself, and wonders whether it has any validity, and we are worse off than ever.

—UAS, 16

Faith

The reviviscences of the Catholic Church, e.g. at the Counter-reformation, do not really give ground for expecting the same in any other religious body. For the Catholic Church keeps the faith; and, though we know charity is greater than faith, faith is a harder virtue to revive.

— DIF, 201

Faith [is an] inalienable part of your make-up; not something which you have got hold of, but something which has got hold of you.

— HS, 154

Faith, then, in its central essence, presupposes a judgment of the intellect, a judgment first that God exists; next that he has revealed himself in Jesus Christ, and finally that the Catholic Church is the accredited vehicle of Christ's revelation, and that what she teaches comes to us, consequently, with that certainty which belongs to the Voice of God.

— ISG, 104

To restore the spirit of faith you must first restore the spirit of charity.

— OCC, 233

With faith, we may save our own souls; we need the *spirit* of faith, much more of it than we have, if we are to save the world.

— OCC, 254

There is, after all, no better way of convincing the world around us that to us religion is something real, than the pertinacity with which we go on building up and developing the external fabric of it in spite of every discouragement.

— OCC, 314

Faith lives on mystery; that is its proper food; without mystery it can only languish.

$$-PAS, 328$$

Man is happy in the long run only when he is giving himself, and so far as he succeeds in giving himself, to something other than himself; only when he is working for a cause or a creed or a personality to which he can devote himself, with some kind of assurance that he is not wasting his time in doing so. And that kind of assurance can only be achieved by faith—if we take faith in its widest, its most human, its least supernatural acceptation.

$$-UAS, 71$$

Faith (Catholic)

So long as we retain the Catholic faith we have always one interest, one loyalty, one enthusiasm in the world to keep us alive. . . . It does commit us to a philosophy; but it does also take us out of ourselves by throwing our reliance on . . . the Personality of Jesus Christ; . . . by identifying us with a movement, whose triumphs are our triumphs, whose anxieties are our anxieties; life can never be dull for us while the Church is still militant, still has a battle to fight and a position to be vindicated.

$$-UAS, 73$$

The Fall

The consequences of the Fall consist not so much in the infliction of certain punishments as in the withdrawal of certain privileges, which privileges were from the first more than man had any strict right to expect. We are not being punished for Adam's sin, but for a race-sinfulness common to him and us.

$$-DIF, 171$$

Fanaticism

A fanaticism negative in its inspiration looks curiously unlovely outside its own circle of devotees.

—EN, 133

Fellowship

Somehow, we do not know why, man is born for fellowship, and the breaking-up of any human circle demands its tribute of tears. By way of fortifying their human hearts, fortifying, perhaps, his own human heart against the strain of this parting, our Lord prays such a prayer as no merely human leader would have ventured to conceive. He prays that the disciples may be one with that very unity which binds together the three persons of the Godhead itself.[1]

—PAS, 235

Fox, George

And [Quaker] Fox, though he knew his Bible and knew how to use it in controversy, was not a man to be tied down to the letter of a text while he had the inner light to interpret it by.

—EN, 147

Margaret Fell, one of Fox's earliest converts, who afterwards married him, writes to him in these terms: 'Our dear father in the Lord . . . our souls doth thirst and languish after thee . . . O thou bread of life, without which our souls will starve . . . O our life, we hope to see thee again, that our joy may be full . . . O thou fountain of life . . . O thou father of eternal felicity.' Was it a very long step from such language to complete apotheosis?

—EN, 160

[1] "That they too may be one in us, as thou, Father, art in me, and I in thee" (Jn 17:21).

Forgiveness

One of the most perfectly constructed lines in English poetry is, "To err is human, to forgive, divine." How perfect is the balance of those words. . . . They enshrine two of the greatest mysteries which, as Christians, we are bound to accept. The doctrine, I mean, that man, being what he is, can rebel against God; and the doctrine that God, being what he is, can forgive man.

—HS, 172–73

Have we forgiven? Nothing is more certain about our Lord's teaching than that God's pardon is conditional on ours; the unmerciful servant forfeits, by one act, his sentence of reprieve.

—OCC, 289–90

Forgiveness is not something which can be bought; those to whom it is offered are bankrupts. It is capital advanced to them, which they are to repay with an interest of tears.

—UAS, 395

Friendship

The people we used to know so well, for whom we once entertained such warm feelings, are now remembered by a card at Christmas, if we can succeed in finding the address. How good we are at making friends, when we are young; how bad at keeping them! How eagerly, as we grow older, we treasure up the friendships that are left to us, like beasts that creep together for warmth.

—PAS, 279–80

Success makes us acquaintance, but only misfortune gives us friendship.

—SPI, 44

G

Gentlemen (English)

The whole legend of the "English gentleman" has been built up on Latin and Greek. A. meets B. on the steps of his club, and says, "Well, old man, *eheu fugaces,* what?", and B. says *"Dulce et decorum est pro patria mori",* and the crossing-sweeper falls on his knees in adoration of two men who can talk as learnedly as that. Nobody can really explain the ridiculous prominence the classics still have in English education except by admitting that what saves them is their snob-value.

—LDD, 265

Germans

And as long as differences of nationality last, Englishmen and Americans will always accuse the Germans of unimaginativeness, of pedantic adherence to principle.

—EN, 421

The Germans have a prodigious name for profundity, only because their language is so ill constructed that a man cannot follow their thoughts. But the Germans will never be anything in philosophy; Sir, they eat too much. A full belly goes with an empty brain.

—LDD, 159

Gnosticism

The starting-point of the Gnostic is this: The world we see about us is such a hotch-potch of good and evil, you cannot possibly attribute the creation of it to one God, and a God who is infinitely good. No, you can only account for the facts by supposing that a whole unseen world of angels exists, much higher than ourselves but not enjoying the perfections of divine Wisdom; between them, as the resultant of ill-balanced forces, these must have produced the world as we know it.

—PAS, 501

God

St Thomas, after proving the existence of God, cites the existence of evil in the world as his *primo videtur quod non;* nor does he attempt to answer the problem, which will never be answered, fully at least, in this world. But Lord Russell has been cramming up his argument against the Goodness of God before he will consider any proofs of his existence; he will not look for God in the things that are made, because he is terrified of finding him.

—BCM, 257

If God does not interfere in history to prove the claims of his Church, I want you first to tell me why he does not interfere in history to prove his own existence!

—DIF, 214

Where there is belief in God's existence, there must be belief in His assistance as well; hope is the natural food of faith. The God of the Deists was a convenient postulate, he was not really an object of worship. . . . True, in the higher walks of mysticism you will come across rare souls who aspire to love God only for what he is, not at all in acknowledgment of what he does for us. But the rank and file of worshippers will demand, always, that God should take an interest in his creatures; he must not be ashamed to be called *their* God. Let him punish them sevenfold for their sins . . . let him deal out sorrow as well as joy. . . . But he must have a personal relation to them, somehow, if they are to have a personal relation to him. The heathen may worship gods who have eyes and see not, have ears and hear not, but that is a calf-love which humanity has outgrown. . . . The God who reveals himself in complete indifference will have less crowded temples than the hidden, silent God who cares.

—*GOD*, 54–55

If you are trying to serve him, even though it is not always a great success; if you are aspiring towards him, keeping your head upstream and taking the strain of being a Christian, then you *are* loving God, and every whisper of doubt that you feel about it comes straight from the devil. If the devil can make you think that you aren't loving God, it's his best hope of persuading you to stop loving God; he has no weapon like despair. It doesn't matter how little enjoyment you get out of your religion, it doesn't matter how little progress you seem to be making in the affairs of your soul; it may all be like dragging a log uphill, every Hail Mary wrenched from you with an effort, but you *are* loving God.

—*LAY*, 38

God (Existence of)

The true lesson of the five proofs, as of all other proofs devised to establish the fact of God's existence, is that we see his face looking down at us from the end of every avenue of our thought; there is no escaping from it. All our metaphysics, play with word-counters and reshuffle our concepts as we will, must necessarily take us back to God. The doubts, the hesitations, come only when human knowledge is suffering from growing pains, when we have not yet sorted out our ideas and integrated, for the hundredth time, our world-picture. Of that inevitability, our own heart-sickness is the best proof. "Lo, all things fly thee, for thou fliest me."

—*GOD*, 113–14

God (Love of)

The love of God, St John tells us, resides not in our showing any love for God, but in his showing his love for us first, when he sent out his Son to be an atonement for our sins. Forget that, and you have forgotten to be a Christian.

—*PAS*, 441

God's Judgment

We can only suppose that God judges with infinite tenderness the opportunities, the temptations, the natural disadvantages, the motives, the struggles, of every soul that has ever lived.

—DIF, 209

God's Mercy

Most of the tall stories you will find in the classical writers are stories of omens and portents, or of punishments inflicted by the gods on people who had defied them. The characteristic of nearly all our Lord's miracles, nearly all those in the Acts of the Apostles, nearly all those in the lives of the saints, is that they were designed to show, not God's power only, but also his mercy. It is to heal the sick, to comfort the bereaved, to relieve the poor, to deliver the unjustly imprisoned, to save those in imminent danger of death, that the Christian miracles for the most part were performed. God wants us to see that he is powerful, but he wants us to see that he is merciful too.

—ISG, 67

Gossip

Are you one of the scandal-mongers, the back-biters? There are few faults that are so often overlooked by the consciences of those who are guilty of them as this, perhaps the most odious. Check yourself the next time it occurs to you to say something disagreeable, and don't say it; ask yourself afterwards what possible good you could have done by saying it.

—OCC, 370

Grace

The cause of all graces, whether bestowed on the Saints or on ordinary Christians, is not their membership of the Church, but the merits of our Lord Jesus Christ. Membership of the Church is rather a condition than a cause, whether of salvation or of sanctity. If the Church were the cause of sanctity, then to find saintly people outside the Church would be as extraordinary as finding people who could maintain life without liquid refreshment.

—DIF, 193

Hearing comes first, faith afterwards; the ears of the soul must be attuned, as it were, to the spiritual music as a preliminary. A man who is deaf can eat and drink and move like the rest of us, but there is a whole world of experience from which he is cut off; not only the world of music, but all the charm of conversation with his fellows. So it is with the soul which has not received justifying grace; it has the full powers of humanity, can perform right and wrong actions, but it is shut off from that whole world of supernatural life in which the regenerate soul moves. The airs of grace beat round it, like sound-waves about the ears of a deaf man, in vain. Even the infant which is brought to the font still belongs to the kingdom of fallen nature. It is fitting that the words "Be opened" should come first.

—*LIG,* 79–80

The further the sinner strays, the more powerful are the motions of grace that woo him back again. . . . You pass easily from one venial sin to another: each time, the habitual grace that is at work in you resists, and you overpower its resistance. The grace does not lessen as the weeks go by, but the habit that is impressing itself on your character becomes more deeply engraved with each succeeding failure. . . . And then, at last, comes the crucial temptation, a temptation to mortal sin; and with it comes grace, we know that, grace sufficient to resist it; a stronger impulse of grace than we have yet known.

—*PAS,* 109–10

You look round at the world, and see sin unpunished and virtue unrewarded, and you would think that God slept, took no responsibility for the harvest of what he has sown; but we know better. He does not, as a rule, interfere with us by outward evidence of his power and clear advertisements of our peril; but within stubborn human hearts, the hearts that despite his messengers and crucify the Son of God afresh, the merciful influence of his grace is still working; still ready to work, if we will intercede for it.

—*PAS,* 112

It is painfully true that small things do matter; and it is in small things that we are always missing the opportunities which grace offers us.

—*PAS,* 136

God never leaves us without sufficient grace to resist a temptation, but where he foresees that we shall succumb he so directs his providence as to form a loving plot for our further advancement, if we will.

$$-PAS,\ 168$$

Gratitude

So slight is the value of human gratitude.

$$-OCC,\ 392$$

How often did our Lord himself publicly offer thanks to God? Only three times, as far as our records enlighten us. He gave thanks to God at ... the feeding of the five thousand and the raising of Lazarus. And he gave thanks to God once more when he was about to perform the greatest of all his miracles; when ... on the night on which he was betrayed, ready to turn the substance of bread and wine into that of his adorable body and blood. In all three gospels ... and equally in the account of which St Paul gives us, that detail is prominent; he gave thanks, and broke the bread; he gave thanks, and bade them drink of the cup.... Even now the traitor is sitting with him at table, and he knows it. But the thought which fills the heart of our divine Lord at that first Mass of Christendom is an overwhelming impulse of gratitude.

$$-PAS,\ 222$$

If you have ever felt gratitude in your life, then you owe it all to God.

$$-UAS,\ 363$$

If ever you have felt, in the contemplation of a sunset or any perfect work of nature or art, ... in the thrill of good news or in the passion of first love, that it was really worthwhile being alive—then that moment was a revelation to you, if you had the heart to understand, of what you owe to the Almighty for having created you.

$$-UAS,\ 363$$

H

Happiness

Man's happiness lies in devoting himself; his success in the offering he can make.

—*OCC*, 28

Hell

Going to hell is going to a place where all the people, not just some people, all the time, not just some of the time, are trying to assert themselves and hating one another.

—*LAY*, 211

"He Must Increase"

To drop more and more out of view, and let others profit by the beginnings we have made and the experience we have won for them; to make way for our children to succeed in the world better than we did, to see our pupils outshine us, or our rivals outstrip us, . . . what a common experience that is in life, what a natural one, and yet, how hard to sit down under it!

—*UAS*, 348–49

Heretics

The enthusiast who thinks very few people will go to heaven ordinarily assumes that he is one of them.

—*EN*, 217

It may be the complete inner conviction of the Calvinist that he is bound for heaven; it may be the warm consciousness of the Wesleyan that his sins are, here and now, forgiven: in either case, there is the feeling that . . . a threshold has been crossed, nature has been supernaturalized. So it is with the more modern enthusiast who tells you that 'his life has been changed'.

—*EN*, 223

Heroism

All very well to say that the Christian martyrs had something better to die for; but it is possible to have a special admiration for people who sacrificed their lives with no hope, or a shadowy hope at best, of a blessed immortality. No, I think most of us will be content to leave these and many other acts of heroism, works done apparently without the grace of Christ, in the hands of the God who made us all and hates nothing that he has made. "There shall never be one lost good"—that is all we can feel certain of.

—*OCC*, 344

Hirelings

We must cut out the hireling spirit altogether—the spirit which fancies itself working for God under a contract, merely under a contract. That's what's the trouble with the hireling; his contract binds him to do this and that, see that this and that doesn't happen, *but he doesn't feel bound to do anything over and above the terms of his contract.*

—*UAS*, 317–18

Hiroshima

If the decision, whether to bomb Hiroshima or not, had lain with a single man, not bound to consult anybody's interests except his own, Hiroshima would probably have been spared. The decision that was taken does not reflect the individual will of President Truman or of any other single human being; it was the work of statesmen, who quite rightly, acted as the representatives of the countries which had given them high office. They had to consider the misery, the loss of life, involved in prolonging a modern war twenty-four hours beyond its necessary limit ... they had to consider the reactions of Allies who were not present. It was not men, in fact, but nations that condemned Hiroshima to suffer.... A whole bundle of human interests is concerned, whenever a decision is made, and these cannot be neglected. Generosity, the gesture of claiming something less than your rights, is to be found in the individual, not in the group.

—GOD, 146–47

History

As I look round the world, the whole of history looks like one vast ruin of pathetic faiths resting on false foundations.

—SLS, 190

God works, not to a five years' or a ten years' plan, but with a purpose that realizes itself slowly through the centuries. The Roman Empire, while it persecuted the Church, was preparing the way for its world-domination. The barbarian inroads, which seemed so destructive, breathed life into a dying civilization. The Reformation itself, by provoking us to jealousy, brought home to us the need for a reformation from within. And, centuries hence, men will find it just as easy to find a meaning and a purpose in what is happening now.

—UAS, 431

Hope

Hope is something that is demanded of us; it is not, then, a mere reasoned calculation of our chances. Nor is it merely the bubbling up of a sanguine temperament; if it is demanded of us, it lies not in the temperament but in the will. . . . Hoping for what? For deliverance from persecution, for immunity from plague, pestilence, and famine . . . ? No, for the grace of persevering in his Christian profession, and for the consequent achievement of a happy immortality. Strictly speaking, then, the highest exercise of hope, supernaturally speaking, is to hope for perseverance and for Heaven when it looks, when it feels, as if you were going to lose both one and the other.

—*GOD*, 115

Human Experimentation

It is true that the Christian world has sometimes discouraged by legislation forms of research which were, or seemed, revolting to human sentiment. Thus it kept in force the old pagan legislation against dissecting human subjects, with its corollary of body-snatching; and it is certain that the same embargo would be placed on any attempt to experiment with the human foetus for research purposes. In much the same way there is a powerful agitation in our own day which would prohibit the use of living animals in the laboratory; an agitation which would have had more chance of success if it had not been for the Christian instinct that man is by right lord of creation. Such handicaps to the advancement of learning may be regrettable from the scientists' point of view, but they are not designed to discourage the advancement of learning. They are imposed in the belief that the suggested procedure is wrong in itself; we are not allowed to do evil in order that good may come of it.

—*BCM*, 269

Humility

All that physical science couldn't tell us, because that doesn't lie within its terms of reference—all that we really mean, and the world really means, why we are here in the world and the world is here in us—we learn only in proportion as we make a surrender of ourselves to God. That is why even philosophy is called the *ancilla*, the handmaid, of theology.

—*OCC*, 375

There is the calculating, affected humility of Uriah Heep; you demean your-self before important people because you know which side your bread is buttered. But real humility, how it shines when it catches the light! The man who can take an affront and feel it is no more than he deserves . . . how we admire such a man, even when we think that he carries his good qualities to a fault! And the reason for our admiration—the historical reason for our admiration—is because we have been told about a God who for us men and for our salvation came down from heaven, and took upon himself the nature of a slave for our sakes.

—*PAS*, 367

Humor

For humour, frown upon it as you will, is nothing less than a fresh window of the soul. Through that window we see, not indeed a different world, but the familiar world of our experience distorted as if by the magic of some tricksy sprite. It is a plate-glass window, which turns all our earnest, toiling fellow-mortals into figures of fun.

—*ESS*, 16

No doubt the psycho-analysts will want us to believe that all humour has its origin in indecency, and . . . that whenever we laugh we are unconsciously thinking of something obscene. But, in fact, the obscene, as its name implies, is an illegitimate effect of humour. There is nothing incongruous in the *existence* of sex and the other animal functions; the incongruity lies merely in the fact of mentioning them. It is not human dignity that is infringed in such cases, but a human convention of secrecy.

—*ESS*, 20

Humorists (Pure)

The pure humorist is a man without a message. He can preach no gospel, unless it be the gospel that nothing matters; and that in itself is a foolish theme, for if nothing matters, what does it matter whether it matters or not?

—*ESS*, 38

Humor vs. Satire

Humour without satire is, strictly speaking, a perversion, the misuse of a sense. Laughter is a deadly explosive which was meant to be wrapped up in the cartridge of satire, and so, aimed unerringly at its appointed target, deal its salutary wound; humour without satire is a flash in the pan; it may be pretty to look at, but it is, in truth, a waste of ammunition. Or, if you will, humour is satire that has run to seed; trained no longer by an artificial process, it has lost the virility of its stock. It is port from the wood, without the depth and mystery of its vintage rivals. It is a burning-glass that has lost its focus; a passenger, pulling no weight in the up-stream journey of life; meat that has had the vitamins boiled out of it; a clock without hands. The humorist, in short, is a satirist out of a job; he does not fit into the scheme of things; the world passes him by.

—ESS, 37

Husband and Wife

I'm afraid the best that most of us really expect them to enjoy is a life-long comradeship. For romance will feed on nothing less satisfying than perfection; and the perfections we human creatures have aren't enough to go round.

—OCC, 223

Huxley, Aldous

Professor Huxley . . . is for ever talking about "values", and telling us about Wordsworth and Beethoven for fear we should mistake him for a materialist. He is not a materialist, but he is a sentimentalist, and he splashes his values all over the place much as you may fix up candles on a Christmas tree; he has no notion where they belong, nor where his admissions lead him to.

—BCM, 251

Huxley, Julian, and H. G. Wells

I have the feeling that if either of the two authors whom I have been discussing were brought into the presence of an actual saint, could sample the atmosphere of a man or woman really eaten up with the idea of God, they would understand better what it is they are trying to take away from us others, when they talk so glibly of religion dissociated from theology. They might be confirmed in the idea that we are the pathetic survivors of an outworn superstition; but they would realize that what they propose to us involves more than a mere change of loyalties. Neither of them really expects to make the irreligious part of mankind more religious; they want to re-orientate the outlook of Christians, under the impression that a good Christian will make a good atheist. I hope they will be undeceived by failure; they will be undeceived, if not, by their success.

−BCM, 246

I

"I"

That "I" which is so covetous of petty superiorities; that "I" which infects even our prayer, even our virtues, making us want to be pure so that we may feel pure, be humble so that we may be free to criticize the pride of others . . . instead of simply wanting God's will to be done in us, and in everybody else. The "I" which takes all its losses and disappointments so badly, asking why *this* should have passed others by, and have been reserved for *me*.

—PAS, 246

Ideals

The people who have no ideals in this world are always dull and generally | unhappy.

—UAS, 72

Ideologies (Modern)

If we were strict utilitarians, we might boast that we were continuing the process of evolution, in a rationalized, human way of our own; we might say that the animal man has learned the secret of co-operation and combination. . . . But we are not strict utilitarians. If we were merely concerned with the greatest good of the greatest number, we should exterminate, painlessly of course, all the irreclaimable criminals, all the lunatics, probably all the weaklings and consumptives. Whereas, if there is any such thing as progress, it's obvious that it means making more and more elaborate efforts to protect those who fall out in the march of life. . . . Theoretically, you can approve of Nietzsche and the Blond Beast. But historically, we have never developed towards that ideal, and we are not developing towards it now.

—SAF, 110

Idleness

Idleness does not necessarily mean continued relaxation. When we have demonstrably wasted an afternoon, we have the grace to be ashamed of ourselves. But there is a subtler form of idleness, which might be called misoccupation; we work hard, but we neglect the priorities. We are engaged upon some task which "can wait", and in the middle of it we remember some other task which we know to be more urgent, but mere *vis inertiae* forbids us to exchange this for that. Or we actually consider the rival claims of two duties, and choose, not the one which is more important, but the one which is less disagreeable. . . . And at the end of a day thus subtly misspent we can lay a flattering unction to our souls; life, we complain, is just "one thing after another". But the real question is whether we did the things in the right order.

—LIG, 133–34

Illuminism

It is the experience of some mystics that their own personality seems more and more to disappear, more and more to be replaced by the divine presence dwelling in them. . . . How far can this process go, before the mystic claims that his own personality has disappeared entirely, to give place to a fresh Incarnation of the Divine Being? We have seen that this difficulty beset the Montanists; 'I am the Father, the Word, and the Holy Ghost', said Montanus.

—EN, 159

Immortality

If it were revealed to me that I was no more and no less immortal than my friend's dog, you would not catch me banking a farthing on eternity.

—CAL, 156

The Incarnation

It is difficult to see how any further revelation of God's goodness, apart from the bare statements about it which the natural theologian can make, would have been possible except by an Incarnation of some sort. To be intelligible to us at all, the things of eternity must be thrown on to the screen of time. A life, a life which involved action, perhaps even a life which involved suffering, was necessary if we were to have a revelation made to us.

—DIF, 156

All theologians teach that our Lord's Life and Passion were not absolutely necessary for our Redemption. That could have been secured by other means; and it was only in order that we might have a proof of the Divine Love and an example of self-sacrifice that the Second Person of the Trinity became Incarnate.

—DIF, 158

He took upon himself the nature of Man, accepted all its inadequacies. . . . He, our Elder Brother . . . became our Victim, the Representative of our sin; hung upon the Cross, and, as if by the shock of that unparalleled encounter, shattered all the barriers that had existed till then—the barrier between God and Man, the barrier between life and death, the barrier between Jew and Gentile. He died, and in his death mankind, as mystically associated with him, died too, so that the old debt incurred by Adam's sin was cancelled.

—HS, 91

The Incarnation, for St Paul, did not mean primarily that God had become *a* man; it meant primarily that God had become *Man,* had infected the human race, as it were, with his Divinity.

—HS, 92

So don't let's think that when the Church teaches us the doctrine of the hypostatic union she is merely using long words for the sake of using long words, merely trying to confuse us. It's not that at all; she is trying to safeguard, as accurately as human language can safeguard, the essential truth of the Incarnation; she only wants to make us realize that when she says God became Man she is not guilty of a metaphor or a piece of pulpit rhetoric.

God did really become Man; was Man, and lay in the manger, was Man, and hung on the Cross, is Man, and has united with himself for ever that human nature he took, humiliated on earth, scarred with the scars of earth; reigns in it, eternally, in heaven.

—ISG, 146

It means . . . God made Man has experienced cold, hunger, thirst, fatigue, sleeplessness, bodily suffering of the most intense kind; that he has known the emotions of love, pity, indignation, joy, grief, and bodily fear; that he has suffered from the neighbourhood of evil, and of the Prince of evil himself; that he has allowed himself to descend into the depths of spiritual desolation; that he has worked, and watched, and prayed, and lived the life of common men. . . . In the bond of that common experience he offers us a human friendship; a friendship which survives neglect and coldness on our part . . . and does not end with death.

—UAS, 109

Ingrates

Like nine lepers who didn't come back to say thank you. . . . We spend most of our time grumbling about the little things that go wrong, and forgetting the enormous majority of things that go right.

—UAS, 374

The Injured

We are always eager to soften by little attentions those whom we have injured.

—BAR, 62

The Inquisition

The Spanish Inquisition ought to be treated as a separate phenomenon. It was not instituted by the Church, but by the Spanish Government, in spite of the protests of the Church; the Church disapproved of secularly conducted Inquisitions on the express ground that they were too harsh, and the Popes tried to dissuade both the Milanese and the Neapolitans from instituting them on the same grounds.

—DIF, 24

Intellect

God wouldn't have given us an intellect, if he didn't want us to think straight.

—UAS, 39

Intellectual Assent

To submit your will to a law outside yourself which has no intellectual meaning for you is to live the life of a vegetable. If you are to regulate your conduct by supernatural sanctions you must have at least the beginnings of a creed, at least the glimmerings of a theology.

—CAL, 40–41

Intellectual

They have substituted for the infallibility of the Church a doctrine of the infallibility of perishable human intellects.

—SLS, 227–28

Irishmen

An Irishman must be a politician; it is a necessity of his nature.

—SAF, 130

Irony vs. Satire

There is, indeed, less contempt in satire than in irony. Irony is content to describe men exactly as they are, to accept them professedly, at their own valuation, and then to laugh up its sleeve. It falls outside the limits of humorous literature altogether; there is irony in Plato, there is irony in the

Gospels; Mr. Galsworthy is an ironist, but few people have ever laughed over Mr. Galsworthy. Satire, on the contrary, borrows its weapons from the humorist; the satirized figure must be made to leap through the hoops of improbable adventure and farcical situation.

−ESS, 31

Israel

The one God, the God who is so spiritual a being that you must not represent him even by a human figure, the God who demands, as the price of his favour, kindliness to the poor, honesty in all your dealings, the avoidance, at least, of gross sensual excess—all that, the dream of the sage, is the common birthright of Israel.

−HS, 64

Israelites

There they stand, then, mustered by their tribes on the fringe of the desert, a new people. A new people, that is the point; that is what they have got to understand. They are not to be like any other nation in the world, because they have not, like the other nations of the world, a history, an ancestral tradition with its roots in the past. It is a nation which has suddenly sprung into being; not by a process of new creation, but by a process of death and resurrection. They are God's peculiar people; his own in a special sense, because he has bought them in by the paschal covenant.

−RFP, 66

J

Jansenism

To be a Jansenist you must always be writing *against* somebody.

—EN, 196

Of all the Jansenist tricks none is more clearly un-Catholic than the readiness with which they assume their neighbour's damnation.

—EN, 203

Jansenism never learned to smile. Its adherents forget, after all, to believe in grace, so hag-ridden are they by their sense of the need for it. *Everything* in the world is wicked.

—EN, 212–13

Jesus Christ

For his delight is to be with the sons of men; those thirty-three years he spent as man in our midst were not a prodigy, isolated and apart; rather they were the characteristic expression in time and in history of the eternal charity that *will* draw near to us, *will* rule in men's hearts, though it be to rule amongst his enemies, *will* come to his own, though his own do not receive him.

—PAS, 317–18

He will divide us into two classes, only two—those who confessed, and those who denied him. He will point us to one of two destinies, only two—to be confessed or to be denied before his Father in heaven. Judge honestly, then, for to him all hearts are open; judge anxiously, for it is you who will sustain the sentence.

—PAS, 382–83

He died that he might institute such means of grace; he died that he might obliterate the curse of sin under which our race laboured; he died that he might encourage us to follow heroically in his footsteps; he died that we might learn how intimate a place suffering has in the economy of our existence here. He died also, that he might assume for our sakes, while he was yet on earth, that Resurrection body whose true home and medium of activity is elsewhere; we should see with our eyes, and our hands should handle, the Word of Life.

—PAS, 400

Jesus, Society of

The Society of Jesus . . . is the home of *lost* causes; what other institution in the world looks back on such a long record of failures that nearly succeeded?

—OCC, 254

The Jews

I simply can't get over the extraordinariness of the Jewish people. I mean, even if you approach the Old Testament without any belief in inspiration, . . . there is something obstinately Providential about the story of the Jews. Even if Christianity had never happened, it would still challenge belief, the way in which this tiny nation has drawn a trail of theology over the face of history; the way in which all its literature, and such superb literature, reduces itself to an epic of the soul.

—HS, 63

Was there ever a people whose history was, to all outward appearance, such a long series of tragedies and of disappointments? But all through their darkest times they had a hope to cling to; a hope founded in the promises made to them and to their forefathers that one day redemption would come to them.

—PAS, 475

Those forty years spent in the wilderness left a permanent mark on the Jewish people. It was, surely, during that period of isolation . . . of separation from their earlier traditions, of consolidation under a single, central leadership, that the Jews attained the fixity of type, the retentiveness of old customs, the capacity for maintaining their culture even in exile, that has marked them to this day. Under the fire of those desert suns the type hardened, like baked clay, and it has retained the mould ever since. In the desert, Israel was undergoing the hard schooling that was to qualify it for the Promised Land, and when it went over Jordan, it went with its characteristics already determined, and its destiny sealed.

—RFP, 89

The Jews have no instinct of colonization; they neither impose on others a culture of their own, nor acclimatize themselves perfectly as the citizens of an alien kingdom. Their stubborn independence, which is their chief religious virtue, is their chief political drawback. And accordingly, not once nor twice in the world's history, the Jewish people has been threatened with extinction by neighbours piqued at the insularity of its outlook, and jealous of its commercial success.

—RFP, 168

The Jewish people was, and is, unique. The Jews alone in the ancient world had preserved the tradition that there is one true God. Oh, I know they were always falling short of that standard, and relapsing into idolatry; but they always came back to their origins, drove out the false idea, and confessed their shortcomings. And if they were unique in their faith, they were unique also in their hope. Alone among the nations of the world, they looked forward to the future instead of looking back to the past; the expected coming of a Redeemer.

—UAS, 30–31

III

That faith and that hope combined with, and helped to form, an intensely nationalistic feeling among them which made it impossible, and (some would say) still makes it impossible to merge them in the common stock of mankind. Ask yourself what an ancient Roman or an ancient Greek, a Babylonian or an Assyrian looked like, and you will have to go to the sculptures in a museum to find out. Ask yourself what an ancient Jew looked like, and you have only got to go to the jeweller's round the corner. They preserved then, as they preserve now, their obstinate nationality.

—*UAS*, 31

Saint John

If it may be said with reverence, what a bad story-teller is St John! ... Nobody, you might say, would have been a worse journalist.

—*PAS*, 216

Saint John the Baptist

He has left us one golden phrase, which should never be far from our minds when we are waiting for our blessed Lord to come to us in holy communion; "he must become more and more; I must become less and less."

—*PAS*, 241

The tragedy of St John is not that he was persecuted, nor that he met a violent death: people built as he was do get persecuted, do meet a violent death: but that he died too soon to witness the glories of the Resurrection, too soon to strengthen and promote the faith of the infant Church.

—*UAS*, 348

Johnson, Dr. Samuel

Johnson will remain a tradition and a legend, for generations of Englishmen to admire. He will be remembered ... as one who was born in a humble station, yet rose, through the editing of several newspapers, into a position of intimacy with rich men. ... If the facts of his life are now mostly disputed, and the authenticity of his works largely denied, that is, after all, but the penalty of having matriculated two hundred years ago—it may as well come now, since it would have had to come sooner or later. "Facts", says the Bishop of Much Wenlock in the current number of his Diocesan Magazine, "are only the steam which obscures the mirror of truth."

—*ESS*, 260–61

Journalists

The newspaper proprietor, while he aspires to be the tyrant of public opinion, must in many ways stoop to be its slave.

—*OCC*, 23

Joy and Sorrow

In proportion as we are good Christians, the world will find us . . . a little removed from its insensate pursuit of pleasures, a little obsessed with thoughts of death and of judgment, a little sceptical about its facile optimisms . . . in proportion as we are good Christians, this seriousness of character will not reflect itself in empty brooding on the wickedness of the world, will not make us morbid, self-centered, disillusioned. Rather, we shall find that Christian sorrow and Christian joy have their roots nearer together than we fancied; that the desire for God's will to be done perfectly in us and in all creatures, which *is* the Christian religion, bears a double fruit of sadness and of gladness. For so it must be, until our earthly Lent is over, and we rejoice for ever in the triumph of the eternal Easter-tide.

—*PAS*, 190–91

Judas Iscariot

Had there to be a Judas Iscariot? No—it was not necessary that our Lord should die at all. But that he should die, and die as he did, was evidently included in the Divine plan. All we can see, surely, is a man created by God with great possibilities for good or evil; a free choice before him between the top of heaven and the bottom of hell. Twelve such men were created and chosen to be Apostles; one of them, freely, made the wrong choice. Somehow, this monstrous abuse of human free will fitted into God's plan. . . . But you must not try to use force (as it were) in solving the mystery, either (*a*) by talking as if Judas' treachery was a lucky accident or (*b*) by talking as if God compelled Judas to be a traitor. *O felix culpa,* the Church says of it; it was a blessed crime—the paradox reflects the mystery.

—OR, 169

Woe unto that man by whom the Son of Man is betrayed.[1] *You are not all clean; One of you shall betray me.*[2] And then the sacrament of the New Covenant is instituted, and it is Judas' last chance. . . . But no, the hardened conscience goes through with it; he receives the saving host to his condemnation, receives the sop which is the special pledge of charity, and with the sop Satan enters into him, and he hurries out into the night. The cares of the world and the love of riches had so strangled the good seed that no root survived even of penitence; he went out into the night, and night went out with him.

—PAS, 162

Judgment

Just as a person who has never felt acute pain is no judge of pain (he knows the meaning of the word, but cannot appreciate its content), so an outlook which is imperfectly supernaturalized is no judge of sin.

—DIF, 67

God reads the secrets of the heart; he is not impressed by successful careers, or by solid earthly achievements; it is our motives, the use we have of our opportunities, small or great, that he will judge. And, not seldom, he will show us that the choice of his predilection fell upon a soul which was never the world's candidate, never the world's hero; he will floodlight with the aura of sanctity some obscure niche in a convent cell or within the walls of a prison.

—OCC, 150

Even when there is no bond of common Christianity, we have a vague respect for a man's religion; he is a Buddhist, yes, but he has got hold of something. To have any respect at all for a man's irreligion—that is much harder. And yet he, too, has got hold of something; he believes, as we do, in logical proof;

[1] Mt 26:24.
[2] Jn 13:10, 21.

believes, as we do, in historical accuracy; hates, as we do, the very name of superstition.

— OCC, 357

All those dark secrets of the human conscience, on which our limited human knowledge finds it so difficult to pass judgment, gave themselves away when the light came into the world. . . . And our Lord could tell us quite truly, that he had come to save the world, not to pass sentence on it. But the people who rejected him thereby passed sentence on themselves.

— PAS, 249

Judgment Day

We know that we shall not all be equal in glory; the equality . . . lies in this, that each soul is fulfilled to its full extent with the delights of God's house. And we know that there can be no murmuring or envying in that manifestation of the sons of God. We shall, I imagine, have no time to say "Who could have thought of seeing you there?" We shall be too engrossed in the reflection, "Who would have thought of seeing me here?"

— PAS, 144

Justice

To the Jew, justice was a state of the soul arising out of, and manifested in, a faithful observance of the law, moral and ceremonial. To the Christian, justice is a state of the soul arising out of baptism, and the act of faith which he makes in baptism.

— TOT, 60

K

Kneeling

Man is the only species in creation to which kneeling is a native posture.

—OCC, 211

Knowledge

Once you start trying to acquire knowledge merely for the sake of knowledge, it's . . . well, strictly speaking, it's the abuse of a faculty.

—LDD, 261

L

Language

Nothing so unites, nothing so divides the human race as the gift of speech.

—UAS, 432

Laughter

Laughter and love are everywhere; in healthy people there is no war between them.

—LIT, 159

Law

If there is any meaning in talking of the laws of nature, it must be that the laws are merely the expression of the will of Something behind the laws themselves.

—SLS, 55

The materialist talks about things being governed by laws, hoping thereby to escape from the notion of a Creator. He neglects to observe, that "law" is a metaphor drawn from human Society. In our loose way of talking, we are ready to say "the Law compels me to do this", "the Law forbids me to do that".

—SLS, 55

Law (Christian)

Christian law, St Paul tells us, is not written on tables of stone, but on fleshly tables of the heart. It is not a code of directions exterior to ourselves, but a spirit with which we are to be imbued, an attitude which we are to assimilate.

—*OCC*, 87

Learning

There is no learning, where men do not rise gladly to their books.

—*LDD*, 113

Life

If it is an accident that our world should be capable of producing life, it is presumably an accident also that it should in fact have produced it, and that that life should have persisted.... the emergence of life from inorganic matter must have been an outside chance, verifiable ... once in how many centuries? And the emergence of animal life from vegetable life is another such chance; what were the odds against the first amoeba ... having a fatal accident? And, once more, the emergence of man from the brute must have been only an outside chance; the odds were all against our leaving the tree-tops, all against our surviving if we did. The existence, then, of man—but for whom the universe would have been meaningless, a play without a spectator—is not merely an accident but a complication of four separate accidents, not to mention the accident which, presumably, brought the universe into existence in the first place. We may be pardoned for asking whether the coincidence is not rather remarkable. Circumstantial evidence, says Holmes, quoting Thoreau, can be very convincing, as when you find a trout in the milk.

—*BCM*, 264–65

As you look back over your life, you will be struck by some odd chain of cause and effect in it, and your mind will be carried beyond that to the first Cause, which is God. You will think of the changes which have passed over you, in body and mind, as the years have passed, with nothing but the frail bridge of memory to connect what you are with what you were, and you will see, as the Agent in those changes, the prime Mover, who is God.

—HS, 18

If there is really anything Providential in the arrangement of the Universe, is it possible that Man should have been put down here with his appetite for truth and beauty, just allowed to serve a kind of apprenticeship, to flesh his teeth on the half-realized beauties and the half-revealed truths of earth, if there were no fuller satisfaction waiting for him elsewhere, to slake the thirst which his earthly experiences have bred in him?

—HS, 47

We are given a lifetime for our probation; so many years, so many weeks, so many days; it will be useless to complain that we were not given more time.

—PAS, 116

The business of our life in this world, after all, is not to leave a mark on it behind us or to take an honoured name away from it with us, but to make our peace with God before he calls us to a better one.

—UAS, 349

If [God] had done nothing else for us, the mere fact that he gave us life alone makes any sort of happiness or any sort of gratitude possible for us.

—UAS, 363

Life (Hidden)

In the pattern of Christian life, whether you study it in the hidden years at Nazareth, or in the history of the saints, or in the ideals of the religious orders, the love of obscurity, of waiting upon God alone and letting the world go its own way without you, is an integral part of sanctity ... we must have a hidden life if we are to cultivate the familiar friendship of almighty God.

119

What greater consolation than to be certain, however little the world knows or understands us, of being known to him?

—PAS, 187

Literature (Modern)

It is easy for the satirist to make fun of us, and how much there is in modern literature which puts us out of conceit with ourselves! Unfortunately, it is only a step from cynicism to despair; the man who has convinced himself that his fellow creatures are all second-rate is content, as a rule, to be second-rate himself.

—OCC, 255

Love

Love isn't something we do, it is something which happens to us; something which gets us down, alters us.

—LAY, 31

Loyola, Saint Ignatius

[This] saint bequeathed, not only to his own institute but to Christendom in general, one legacy for which, even if he had left no Order behind him, Christendom would owe him eternal gratitude—the Spiritual Exercises.

—OCC, 66

Luther, Martin

In Luther the humanist had killed the mystic; instead of creating that ideal church which is the recurrent dream of enthusiasm, he had become the father of a national establishment whose gross humours his theology of imputed righteousness did nothing to purge.

—EN, 398

Lying

I can't say I have ever noticed any difference between Catholics and other (well-intentioned) people in this matter. . . . St. Thomas thought the essence of a lie was its being a sin against reason (not necessarily in its taking the other chap in), and therefore all sorts of ingenious ways were devised for making your statement correspond with the truth and yet not giving away the secret you were bound to keep . . . in real life I don't think Catholics ever equivocate, because it demands such a confounded lot of ingenuity if you are to do it on the spur of the moment. They just lie, as Protestants do, when telling the truth would have disastrous consequences; schoolboys and politicians, of course, especially, and I don't suppose God holds it against them much.

—*OR,* 146–47

121

M

Machinery (Modern)

A fate with which the modern age is sometimes threatened by its prophets is that of becoming enslaved to its own machinery. But the remedy lies with ourselves; we only capitulate to the machine if we allow suggestion from without to produce in us a mechanized habit of mind.

—GOD, 16

Magic

It is bad anthropology to regard magic as the ancestor of religion. It would be truer to say that magic is the ancestor of science.

—HS, 2

Man

Only Man has dignity; only man, therefore, can be funny. Whether there could have been humour even in human fortunes but for the Fall of Adam is a problem which might profitably have been discussed by St. Thomas in his *Summa Theologiae,* but was omitted for lack of space.

—ESS, 19

Ultimately the spirit of man is the arbiter of his happiness; men will be merry or sad according as they have found their right place or their wrong place in the scheme of things; and peace between nations, peace between classes, will come only when man is at peace with himself, and at peace with God.

—*OCC*, 12

Man (Common)

He has been standing at a point in the road where modernism opens out on one side, and, if you like, complete intellectual suicide on the other. He is looking nervously down each of these in turn; the one thing that never seems to occur to him is ... to go straight on. Let him trust orthodox tradition to determine what he is to believe, *and common sense to determine what is orthodox tradition.*

—*SLS*, 216

Man (Ill-used)

Those who think themselves ill-used suddenly begin to take a far higher view of their own merits and motives than any they had entertained hitherto; as if the glow of indignation which they feel lit up a kind of aura about their heads.

—*BAR*, 79

Man (Just)

The best that can happen to him, the just man, is that he should be taken away, lest wickedness should alter his understanding, or deceit beguile his soul.

—*OCC*, 26

Man (Simple)

The less we cling to worldly enjoyments, the more we accustom ourselves to do without worldly enjoyments, the better chance we shall have of cultivating that true simplicity which is the simplicity of the saints.

—*OCC*, 98

I think if you asked me who was the simplest person I have ever known I should mention the name of one of the cleverest men of our generation, Mr G. K. Chesterton, [who said] somewhere that, if you find a man lying dead under the sofa, you explain the situation to other people by saying: There is a man lying dead under the sofa; you don't say: There is a man of considerable refinement lying dead under the sofa. On such occasions you keep to the essential facts; and that is what simplicity means, to keep to the essential facts; not just at moments, but all your life.

—OCC, 98

Man and Citizenship

The great generality of men become good subjects but not, in any real sense, good citizens. They vote, they pay their taxes, they obey the orders of Government departments, they assist the police, under suggestion from without; they do not contribute anything of their own, their own sense of need or experience of life, towards the formation of a general will; they acquiesce in that general will, which is formed by a governing class of experts.

—BCM, 10–11

Man and Creation

Whether we take the first chapter of Genesis, or the speculations of scientists, for our guide, we have to recognize that the last in the order of time is first in order of importance. The last species, it would seem, to appear on earth, man, is self-evidently, the crown of all that work of creation.

—RFP, 35

Man in Exile

Man is born for eternity, and the horizons of a fallen world are too little for him. Always he tries, and fails, to express himself fully in his earthly surroundings, like some noble beast in captivity. . . . The lover feels, in his first flush of happiness, as if his love was something immortal, indestructible, only to see his romance fade into commonplace. The artist hails the inspiration that has come to him as something almost divine; once it has been committed to paper or to canvas, it no longer contents him. Always we are striving after the unattainable,

124

and achieving the imperfect. Man—fallen man—is a misfit, an exile from his true country. It is that note of exile which has imposed itself, from the first ages, on the language of the Christian Church.

—*PAS*, 276

Marriage

Part of God's design for the sanctification of your soul is the influence which husband or wife is going to have on you.

—*HS*, 200

We still celebrate a marriage with all the old formalities, the bridesmaids . . . and the wedding-cake and . . . the rest of it, but isn't it true that a great many . . . do not really mean what they used to mean when they enter upon that holy contract? They used to mean what they said, when they uttered the words "till death do us part"; now, those words have become for many people a mere legal formality, and marriage is hardly looked upon as more than an experiment.

—*OCC*, 194

Martyrs

This principle, that a death is needed as the gateway to a resurrection, is verified not only in our Lord's life but in the life of his saints. Above all, in that of the martyrs.

—*OCC*, 201

Martyrs (English)

Can you imagine what confidence in God it must have needed for Blessed Cuthbert Mayne, Blessed Edmund Campion, and the long line of martyrs that followed them . . . ? To stand in hourly peril of their lives; to be outlaws when they set foot in England, forfeited criminals when they said Mass, . . . to wander about by unfrequented ways, ill-clad, ill-fed, ill-housed, to hide for their lives . . . they could have borne all that. But to see the Faith, for all their efforts, gradually losing its hold, and persecution achieving its miserable object; to see soul after soul . . . wearying of the long struggle against an unrelenting enemy, and either conforming to a heretical Church, or losing

their faith in religion altogether; to fight almost always and almost everywhere a losing battle—*that* needed confidence in God.

—OCC, 105

The Mass

The priest doesn't simply recall before God the needs of the people who are
there in church, and the needs of the people they are interested in; you
suddenly find that this Mass, your Mass, is being offered for all faithful people,
all over the world . . . it isn't *a* church any longer, it's *the* Church, the holy
Catholic Church, that bounds your horizon, and what is happening there is
not *a* Mass, it's *the* Mass, the one sacrifice that is going on all over the world,
of which this Mass, your Mass, is only the pin-point, focused at a particular
moment of time, within a particular determination of space. Your family
worship is not merely that of the parish; it's the worship of the whole
Christian family, and you are there with the Hottentots and the Laplanders,
children of the same family, met round the same table.

—PAS, 264–65

The sacrifice of the Mass is a mystery, and perhaps its relation to the sacrifice
on the cross is the most mysterious thing about it. Only this is certain, that the
victim who is there presented to the eternal Father for our sakes is the dying
Christ; it is in that posture that he pleaded, and pleads, for our salvation,
atoned, and atones, for the sins of the world. We herald that death in the holy
Mass, not as something which happened long ago, but as something which is
mystically renewed whenever the words of consecration are uttered. From the
moment of his death on Calvary until the time when he comes again in glory,
the dying Christ is continually at work, is continually available. It is in this
posture of death that he pleads for us, when the Mass is offered.

—PAS, 269

The Mass does not add to Calvary, does not multiply Calvary; it is Calvary,
sacramentally multiplied . . . it is Christ continuing what Christ began.

—PAS, 319

Those who are not of our religion are puzzled sometimes, or even scandalized, by witnessing the ceremonies of the Mass; it is all, they say, so mechanical. But you see, it *ought* to be mechanical. They are watching, not a man, but a living tool . . . all in obedience to a preconceived order—Christ's order, not ours. The Mass is best said . . . when it is said so that you do not notice how it is said.

—*PAS*, 342–43

Materialism

It is materialism that depresses our modern outlook—not merely as a philosophy held by certain people, but as a lurking temptation in our own minds. We are tempted to think of man as only a very little better than the beasts, a superbeast which is able . . . to be conditioned into thinking the thoughts we want it to think. Against that, we have to remind ourselves that man was created only a little lower than the angels; if he stoops, it is only because the pattern of his nature has been spoiled. And to see, in a historical context, the pattern of that nature unspoiled, may be possible only to the eyes of faith, but it is a sight worth having.

—*LIG*, 88

The Materialists

The materialist may put up a case for saying that man does not matter; but if he proves his case it is quite certain that nothing else matters; he should be called an immaterialist for his pains.

—*CAL*, 91

Matter and Spirit

There is no more puzzling riddle for a philosopher to solve than the relation between matter and spirit, between the world which meets our eyes and the eyes with which we look out on it.

—*OCC*, 53

Media Authority

Why is it that nowadays, in discussing the weather prospects, people will always tell you, "the wireless says" this and that? The wireless has no access to private information about the weather, any more than about the Stock Exchange. It only gives you the weather report which you will see in the paper to-morrow, and you are no better off for knowing whether it will rain during the night, unless you are a burglar by profession. But, since weather reports were broadcast, people not only quote them more but believe them more (though they are as inaccurate as ever) than they did in the Newspaper Age; conveyed through space, the information seems somehow to come from the horse's mouth, and is dutifully recorded.

—BCM, 17–18

I say then that the wireless not merely encourages us, from the nature of its machinery, to accept a common culture at second hand from the experts and semi-experts who are selected to talk to us; it predisposes us to listen attentively to anyone who will tell us that we live in a scientific age, and must perforce revise our views, not merely of nature but of human life, that we may be able to call them "scientific".

—BCM, 18

Media Bias

The directors of wireless programmes are selecting all the time what it is important that we should hear, and what view of it ought to be presented to us; with no corrective, save the fear of angry letters from subscribers—and these come, as anybody knows who is accustomed to receiving letters from strangers, from the less balanced portion of mankind. Go to the root of the situation, and you find that whereas the newspaper editor is a skilful demagogue, the director of programmes is a dictator.

—BCM, 13–14

Medicine Men

The medicine man is not the forerunner of the priest, he is the forerunner of the scientist.

—HS, 180

Mediocrity

The man in the parable will have argued that, where all were so ill-attired, his ordinary rags would pass muster. So we, in our careless moments, are encouraged by the indifferent morals of our neighbors to imagine that our own second-best will be enough. And we pronounce the formula, inexcusable in both worlds, "That'll have to do."

—*LIG*, 26

Memorials

Wherever you read about a "memorial" in the Old Testament, it means that you are reminding God of something; that we men, so easily forgetful, so soon forgotten, are prompting the memory of a God who never forgets. Human workmanship, of crumbling stone or discoloured bronze, is to challenge the watchful eye of Eternity.

—*OCC*, 273

Mencken, H. L.

When you are writing about history there is always the chance that some reader will come along who can correct your facts; if you are Mr Mencken, it is almost certain that some reader will come along who can correct your facts.

—*BCM*, 35

I do not know whether Mr Mencken talks on the wireless, but he has caught the method to perfection; he dazzles by excess of light, nauseates the intellectual digestion with a surfeit of facts, and leaves the reader, from sheer weariness, disinclined to hear the word "religion" ever mentioned again.

—*BCM*, 141–42

He is a neo-Pagan, pure and simple; his quarrel with the Catholics is that they abominate birth-prevention, his quarrel with the Protestants, that they have introduced Prohibition. He is a pagan, even, to the extent of having an undisguised contempt for democracy.

—*BCM,* 147

The *Treatise on the Gods* leaves the reader with the impression that Mr Mencken does not like clergymen. He does not dislike them because they preach doctrines which are untrue; he will have it that their religion is untrue, because he dislikes them.

—*BCM,* 152

Mercy (Divine)

If the majesty of God is infinite, a deliberate offence to that majesty is infinite in its gravity, and therefore in its consequences; that a creature which deliberately turns its back on and insults its Creator has thereby chosen unhappiness for itself. We are so accustomed to the frequency with which this happens that the outrageousness of the fact is lost upon us. In a sense the difficulty is rather to understand the mercy of God than his justice.

—*DIF,* 53

He hangs there, with all the weight of a world's tragedy upon his shoulders, our sins the nails that fasten him, our sorrows his crown. Yet he has time, even then, for this one penitent; will suffer this one distraction to interfere with the perfect prayer in which he offers his death to the eternal Father.

—*OCC,* 394

It is theologically indefensible to say of any man, Nero, for example, or Mahamet, "That man will go to hell"; we've no right, even in the extreme case, to despair of God's infinite mercies.

—*UAS,* 79

The Mind

The fact is that this universe which is made up of irrational dust bears, nevertheless, the stamp of reason marked upon it; and that man, unique among the creatures, has a reasoning faculty which is akin, evidently, to that higher and immaterial order. Alone among the creatures, man can look back upon himself and become the object of his own thought; can distinguish the world he knows from himself as knowing it. And in the exercise of that faculty, at however low a level, he transcends the limits of mere matter and makes himself one with that higher order of which matter is only the inadequate expression.

—*LAY*, 14

The Lord God breathed in his face the breath of life. Not animal life merely; the animals had been created already. There is nothing to tell us how long the animals had been in existence in a manless world. . . . But this is certain, that with the creation of man's intellectual soul the world, and not the world merely but the whole material universe, culminated and found a meaning. Without that, suns and stars and earth and sea were like a play without an audience. Creation lay there, a vast possibility of experience, with no human intelligence to experience it. Man came, and with man a new kind of life, intellectual life. Man came, harvesting his impressions by memory, reproducing them by imagination, . . . man came, with speech, and laughter, and wonder, and the power to organize a society and to hand down his hardly learned lessons to posterity. . . . And until a soul first looked out from human eyes, creation was only half finished. The play was there, the audience was wanting.

—*RFP*, 3

You must believe, sooner or later, in a Mind which brought mind into existence out of matter, unless you are going to sit down before the hopeless metaphysical contradiction of saying that matter somehow managed to develop itself into mind.

—*UAS*, 8

The point is that order exists in the Universe, and . . . it is logically impossible to conceive of order existing without a Mind. And if we denied the existence of that Mind, and went on thinking about it hard, it wouldn't be very long, I fancy, before most of us would go out of our own.

—*UAS*, 8

131

People who like to use sham-scientific language will not be slow to tell you that the processes of the mind are only a function of the brain. That word "function" is a glorious piece of mumbo-jumbo; it means, in that connection, exactly nothing whatever.

—*UAS*, 9

The Mind (Modern)

The great argument used now against any theological proposition is not, that it is untrue, or unthinkable, or unedifying, or unscriptural, or unorthodox, but simply, that the modern mind cannot accept it.

—*SLS*, vii

If the modern mind is really progressive in politics, it will necessarily be, so far, out of touch with Christianity, and not with Christianity only, but with religion as such, from the mere force of its impatience of other-worldliness.

—*SLS*, 3

The Mind and Matter

The waggling of my tongue, and the twitching of your ears, do subserve an end, though it may not be a very important end, by making it possible for me to transfer my thoughts to your intelligence. But it would be ridiculous to imagine that my thoughts exist for the purpose of making my tongue waggle, or your ears twitch. That which exists for the sake of something else must have less value, in the ultimate nature of things, than that for the sake of which it exists. Pills exist for the sake of health, not health for the sake of pills; which means that health is a more important thing than pills, and so on. And therefore, just in proportion as mind is useless to matter, in that proportion it claims to be a more worth-while thing than matter. So the materialist's boomerang has come back and hit him in the face.

—*ISG*, 12–13

If you are accepting an invitation to dinner, but are anxious to go on to a meeting or a concert or something at nine, you end up your note, "I hope it won't matter if I go just before nine", or "I hope you won't mind if I go just before nine." The sense is, in either case, I hope there is no objection to my going before nine. But we have these two colloquial ways of expressing the same idea, and we give a slightly different twist to the sentiment according as we choose one or the other. When we say, "I hope it won't matter", we hope that it will not transgress against the code of politeness in general. When we say, "I hope you won't mind", we hope it is not the kind of action which will tread on the corns of that particular person. It is only things, you see, which matter; it is only persons who mind.

—*ISG*, 14–15

The English language is not generally supposed to be a good one for expressing philosophical thoughts. And yet as far as I know English is the only language which turns *mind* into a verb and *matter* into a verb. And more than that, although both usages are little better than slang, I think they have a delicate exactness of meaning. Mattering is really connected with what we mean by matter, and minding is really connected with what we mean by mind.

—*UAS*, 12

Miracles

The divine miracles, as we understand them, are exceptional favours, bestowed [by God] here and there now and then . . . to remind us that we are after all his children. He does not perform them as a rule to order, unfailingly, in answer to some special effort on our part. There are exceptions to that rule; the blood-miracles of Naples and the surrounding country for example, if they are miracles indeed. But in the ordinary way he does mean miracles to be the exception, not the rule. . . . That is what is the trouble with these modern devotees of miracle . . . they make it the rule, not the exception. They want us to believe that there is no such thing as pain, that it cannot be God's will for a human being to suffer. They want us to believe that there is no such thing as death, no plunge into the mysteries of the unknown. And that is not our philosophy, nor is it a human philosophy at all; we cannot believe that God countenances it, whatever manifestations may accompany it.

—*ISG*, 72–73

In a word, God is not governed by his laws, but he does, normally, govern the world according to laws. What is there to prevent his suspending the laws, as the judge may suspend a human law for the sake of equity?

—*SLS*, 60

The idea that God cannot go beyond his own fiat is proper to materialists, who believe in no God, Deists, who believe in a God who has ceased, for practical purposes, to exist, and Pantheists, who think of God as so wholly shut up within his creation that he could not, without contradiction of his own being, violate the order of it.... Surely their root difficulty is, not that God could not do miracles, but that he would not do them.

—*SLS*, 60–61

We believe Christianity in spite of the miracles which it involves, not because of the miracles which involve it.

—*SLS*, 63

No doubt hundreds of miraculous stories are pure inventions, but it is only by a gaping undistributed middle that we could use this as an argument against all miracles, even if it were proved: we might as well say that all relics are necessarily spurious, because some have been faked, or that there never were any Christian martyrs, because stories of martyrdom were sometimes written from a merely literary point of view.

—*SLS*, 66

Miracle cannot be probable or improbable; it is either possible or impossible.

—*SLS*, 84

The characteristic of nearly all our Lord's miracles, nearly all those in the Acts of the Apostles, nearly all those in the lives of the saints, is that they were designed to show, not God's power only, but also his mercy. It is to heal the sick, to comfort the bereaved, to relieve the poor, to deliver the unjustly imprisoned, to save those in imminent danger of death, that the Christian miracles for the most part were performed.

— UAS, 48

Miracles (Gospel)

It is extraordinary the way people will tell you that they believe the Gospel, but not the Gospel miracles. If you ask them what they mean by the Gospel, they will tell you that there was a man called Jesus of Nazareth who went about doing good. When they say that, bring them up short by asking them what good he did? Oh, he was gentle, he was considerate, he was forgiving. But where do you hear that he ever gave money to the poor, or nursed the sick, or comforted the mourner, or buried the dead, or visited anybody in prison? Nowhere; he may have, but the Gospels tell us nothing about it. When we say that our Lord went about doing good, we mean that he healed the sick, raised the dead, and so on; that very habit of "doing good" which is the first thought the mention of our Lord's name calls up to us, is, when you come to think of it, a habit of performing miracles. You can't get on without the miracles; the whole story goes to pieces.

— ISG, 66

Modernism

The vice of modernism lies, not in this or that false statement, but in its general attitude about belief. Catholic modernism claimed, and modernism outside the Church implies (without putting it sturdily into words, like Tyrrell), that the defence of Catholic tradition on historical grounds is useless; we ought to accept the fact that a tradition may be historically false, yet spiritually true.

— DIF, 232

It assumes that the truths of the Christian religion, instead of being a set of truths handed down once for all, which it is the duty of the Church to maintain and to teach, are in some way dependent on, and capable of being revised by, the ordinary Christian believer. The principle of democracy has been grafted on to the notion of conciliar authority, and the result of that is Modernism in the making.

— OCC, 178

A good part of the reason why modern critics associate Gospel eschatology with a defect of knowledge is precisely because they have no eschatology of their own. The difficulty with them is not really so much that the Final Cataclysm did not take place at such and such a date, as the fact that they do not believe in a final cataclysm at all.

—SLS, 109

Utilitarianism is based on a principle, the principle of Utility; Monophysitism is based on a dogma, the dogma of a single Nature; but Modernism, like Latitudinarianism, is based on a tendency, the tendency to be up to date. It is an affection of the soul.

—SLS, 214

Modernism (The Beginning of)

You misinterpret the lack of faith in others as a need of intellectual conviction, and try to trim the sails of your theology accordingly.

—SPI, 61–62

Modernists

The Modernist is compelled to say to his congregation, "Just you keep quiet, and *we will tell you what the truth is when we have found out about it.*" The traditionalist can say, "Here is the Truth, written down for you and me in black and white; I mean to keep it, and defend it from attack: will you rally round it? Will you help me?"

—SLS, 229

Moderns

Contradict the moderns, and they pillory you as an obscurantist. Anticipate them, and they suppress you in the interests of their own copyright.

—BCM, 175

The trouble with ... all the moderns, is that [they] prefer vagueness to mystery.

—*DIF,* 179–80

Modern Times

The times in which we live have, increasingly, the effect of depersonalizing us, of making each of us feel a mere unit in the population. Your dust-bin is just like everybody else's dust-bin; the milk-bottles at your door are indistinguishable from the milk-bottles next door; your chimney-pots are just like everybody else's chimney-pots.... The number of your car, the number of your telephone, the number of your income-tax return, they all label you as a unit, not a person; not Mr. or Mrs. or Miss So-and-so, but Number So-and-so.... People come round and ask whether you want capital punishment abolished ... and your name goes down with several hundreds of thousands of people, a cross-section of the population. You will do as well as anybody else, anybody else will do as well as you. You are not a person any longer.

—*LAY,* 4–5

The whole tendency of the human race is away from consecutive thought. The brain is being sacrificed to the senses, as the cinema replaces the theatre and broadcasting obviates the necessity for conversation. The literature which sells is literature which involves a minimum of thought for its digestion; the religion which appears to commend itself to the masses is a sort of pulpy morality from which all intellectual considerations are jealously excluded. Cross-word puzzles have replaced the search for Truth by an endless chase after synonyms. Any challenge to abstract thought or reflection upon first principles is met by a torrent of catchwords and ready-made journalisms which either obscure thought or obviate the necessity for it.

—*OTO,* 170–71

Modesty vs. Humility

Modesty is only the disinclination to hear our own praises sounded above those of other men; by humility man learns that simply because he is man he is nothing.

—*OCC,* 33

Monuments

It is not merely a reminder, to jog our own treacherous memories when they turn away impatiently from contemplating the past. It is also a monument, designed to inspire a generation yet unborn with some passing thrill of emotion.

—OCC, 275

More, Saint Thomas

And had he lived, [the Anglicans] would be telling us, [he]... would certainly have thrown in his lot with the Reformers, with Cranmer and Cromwell... as an old man, he would have helped to build up the sonorous language of the Anglican prayer-book. All that they would be saying, were it not for the unfortunate fact that he died a Roman Catholic, died because he saw that you could not be a Catholic without being a Roman.

—OCC, 119

Never was a man more humble about his own opinions, when they were merely opinions of his own.

—OCC, 123

Mosaic Law

The law showed us what was the right thing to do, without bringing us the grace which would enable us to do it; revelation without illumination. To prove his point, St Paul gives you in the Romans that terrible chapter which describes the soul, unbefriended by grace, seeing at every turn what is the right thing to do, and doing just the opposite... The law didn't justify us; it found us sinners, and left us not only sinners but transgressors; that is the long and short of it.

—PAS, 495

Mysteries (Christian)

The Christian mysteries transcend human thought. But they do not contradict human thought; they cut across our experience just at those points where it is impossible to say "This or that is impossible" because human thought, even in interpreting ordinary human experience, finds in it, at those points, an insoluble mystery. Take the mystery of Transubstantiation. Impossible, you say, that the substance of a thing should be changed into a different substance while the accidents remain unaltered. No, you have no right to say that that is impossible; because the whole relation between substance and accidents is itself a kind of natural mystery; it is a thing which eludes our thought. . . . You are up against the whole puzzle of the relation of universals to particulars, which people have wrangled about for more than twenty centuries, and still haven't arrived at a unanimous conclusion. It is just there, just where "the wheeling systems darken, and our benumbed conceiving soars" that a Voice comes in from the other world and says "This is my Body."

—*ISG*, 142–43

Mystery

People talk as if definition was an attempt to abolish mystery. But actually it is the other way: theological mystery depends for its existence upon the hard outlines of definition.

—*DIF*, 180

Isn't it rather too much of a coincidence that the mysteries of the Christian religion should match, so accurately, the hesitations of human thought?

—*HS*, 161

Mystery and Satire

Mystery and satire are irreconcilable bed-fellows, since it is essential to the one that the reader should be in the dark, essential to the other that the reader should be in the secret.

—*OTO*, 233

Mystic as God Incarnate

Catholic mysticism is protected from . . . delusions, because we know that the union of the Divine and the Human in our Lord was a hypostatic union, a union of two Natures under a single Person; whereas the most highly privileged of the saints can only enjoy a mystical union with God, the human personality remaining unabridged.

—*EN*, 159

Mysticism

Mystical union is not the drop falling into the stream, but the key fitting into the lock.

—*SLS*, 155

Christian mysticism claims its superiority over Oriental mysticism precisely because its ultimate goal is that of complete harmony between two different persons, not the absorption of one personality into another. The goal of ordinary human love (in spite of the poets' language) is not identity, but correspondence. And it is in complete correspondence between his heart and the Heart of Jesus that the Christian looks forward to that full fruition of love, which is his hope for eternity.

—*SLS*, 155

Mystics

No writers have insisted more strongly than the mystics themselves on the fact that ecstasy can be counterfeited by diabolic influence, or even by hysteria. One of the privileges of sanctity, it is not necessarily a mark of sanctity.

—*EN*, 28

Our Lord's closest friends have not been learned people who knew how to argue in favour of his religion, but simple people who have known how to live it. Not to know about God, but to know God — that is the ambition of the mystic.

—*HS,* 112–13

N

Neighbors

Is it for you, the beneficiary for all time of that unique act of charity, to haggle over obligations and weigh out mercy with a balance? The world is your neighbour. Your enemy is your neighbour. The people who annoy you, bore you, rub you up the wrong way, are your neighbours. Whoever needs your help, however unworthy, however ungrateful, however unwilling, that man is your neighbour.

—PAS, 85

Neopaganism

There is a new kind of paganism springing up, in these days when men ... fashion a God for themselves after their own imaginations. The danger, now, is not polytheism but pantheism. Men will agree with us that God exists, ... but when we examine their meaning more closely we find that they do not think of him as almighty, as existing before all worlds and independent of all other existence besides himself. Rather, they will tell you that ... God and the universe form one single being; God is the soul, and the universe the body; it is no more possible to think of God as existing without the universe than to think of the universe as existing without God. That is the modern blasphemy we have to encounter.

—OCC, 190

New Age

This kind of suggestion—that we belong to a new period, that a line has been drawn across the page of history—insinuates itself very easily into the mind, and with formidable effects. Not for nothing did the statesmen of the French Revolution set about revising the calendar; these tiny details in the build-up of our world-outlook have power to prejudice the mind. If we are going to think of our age as wholly discontinuous with the past, and to boast of it, we shall not even have the gloomy satisfaction of profiting by experience.

—*GOD*, 12

New Covenant

Under the New Covenant, Man is still on his probation; God seems to sleep while the seed grows up and ripens for the harvest; but, once the doom is pronounced, once soul and body are parted, there is no second chance for the soul that was found unprovided with the oil of sanctifying grace; nor will there be any opportunity to complain that our grace was insufficient, any more than for the Jews who neglected to hear Moses and the prophets. To prepare ourselves for that dreadful hour is man's business in the world, not to labour for profits here.

—*PAS*, 140

New Start

There are so many occasions in life, aren't there, when we say to ourselves, "Now I really shall be able to make a new start"? We leave school; of course, all our troubles will disappear now. We go into business; now the world shall see what we are made of. We get married. . . . We rise to a position of responsibility; now, our chance has come. We grow rich, and have more opportunities of leisure. . . . We retire from active work; now . . . we can live as we would wish to die. Yes, but tell me, is there really all that difference between one stage and the next?

—*PAS*, 395

New Testament

With all the libraries that have been written about the Synoptic problem, I have never heard of any critic who tried to shew that the general picture given of Jesus Christ in these private sources was different from that given in the common source. Isn't that rather remarkable, except on the assumption that in outline, at any rate, the whole thing is genuine?

—HS, 84

Nonbelievers

Nobody goes to hell except through his own fault; and therefore, if and in so far as their unbelief is not their fault, I believe that God will make allowances for them.

—DIF, 209

"No Salvation Outside the Church"

If you are asked, "What is the exact meaning of the maxim, *No salvation outside the Catholic Church*", what are you to say about it? The simplest way to put it, I think, is this—there is no other religious body in the world except the Catholic Church which makes a supernatural contribution to a man's chances of salvation. He may receive natural help from some other source; his conscience may be stirred by the preaching of the Salvation Army, or he may learn a useful habit of mental prayer from the Buchmanites, or his sense of worship may be stimulated by the beauty of the ceremonies which he witnesses at the Church of the Cowley Fathers. But there's only one religious body whose membership, of itself, tends to procure our salvation, and that is the Catholic Church. If anybody is saved without visible membership of it he is saved, not because he's an Anglican, not because he's a Methodist, not because he's a Quaker, but for one reason only—because he is a Catholic without knowing it.

—ISG, 118–19

Novelists (Modern)

In the old days, before the 1914 war, if you bought a novel you expected it to have a plot; the interplay of various human actions would lead up to a situation, a *dénouement*, breathlessly awaited, artistically inevitable. If it didn't, you demanded your money back.... Then the novelists found out ... that you could fool the public by giving it a novel which hadn't got a plot at all.... And you could boast that you despised novels with plots in them; just as people who can't afford to keep a gardener let their beds all go to grass nowadays, and pretend that they prefer it that way.

—*LIT,* 150

O

Obedience

The virtue of obedience, nowadays, is a specifically Catholic virtue. The Protestant or half-believing or unbelieving world around us does not understand that it is a virtue at all.

—OCC, 81

Obedience (Tests of)

There are, I suppose, three fruits of obedience, three tests by which the habit may be known, all of which we can read in Abraham's career. One is the instinct of preferring not to choose for yourself, of feeling safer when the choice is left to another. The second is patience when your work seems to go unrewarded. And the third is a willingness to sacrifice your most cherished hopes, however necessary they may seem to the fulfilment of God's purpose for you, if it becomes clear that God has some other plan for you instead.

—RFP, 26–27

Obedience and Authority

The Protestant, in fact, thinks that obedience exists because without it there could be no authority. The Catholic is more likely to tell you that authority exists because without it there would be no obedience.

—OCC, 81

Opinion (Expert)

Conspiracies of expert opinion in the Press have long cowed us into silence by assuring us that this or that was the opinion of all progressive, enlightened and humane men. There fell a shadow over our debates when somebody broke in with the magic phrase "It says in the paper that . . . " *It* says, much in the same sense as "it rains", "it snows"; there is a general tide or body of opinion that forms itself without reference to us loafers in the public house, inevitable as the weather and sometimes as incalculable. In *the* paper; we are not told that the item in question was shoved in by a sub-editor at the last moment and rests on the authority of a wretched journalist who lives in fear of offending Lord So-and-so; "the" paper has acquired, from the vast circulation it enjoys, a unity and a uniqueness attributed, by a less enlightened age, to the Bible. . . . "The" paper; as we say "the" wireless.

—BCM, 12–13

Opportunities Lost

What I'm thinking of at the moment is the opportunities which take us by surprise, don't give us time to examine our motives like that. And I think there are three reasons, in the main, for which we are apt to lose these opportunities. One is want of imagination. One is want of alacrity. And one is want of courage.

—LAY, 140

Ordeals and Vigils

What a noble word is the word "ordeal"—the judgement of heaven, men exposing themselves to great dangers in the confidence that Providence will protect their innocence! But now, if a lift sticks on the tube, all the passengers in it are idiotically described as having undergone an "ordeal" in the papers next morning. And the headline in the next column is something about a "vigil", which calls up to your mind pictures of a knight watching over his arms before the altar of a church, but refers, you find, to a lot of people who got up at five in the morning to queue up at the box-office of a new play.

—LAY, 66

Order

Order is the cipher by which Mind speaks to mind in the midst of chaos.

—*ISG*, 4–5

Oxford

You might as well expect movement in a dead body.

—*LDD*, 165

Oxford philosophy is like a running sore. . . . If it were to close up, it would simply fester.

—*LDD*, 219–20

A kind of isolation hospital, in which the English nation was well advised to segregate all the people who were intelligent enough to prove a nuisance if they went into public life.

—*LDD*, 243

Oxford, of all places in the world, is the one most apt to carry you along tranquilly in its own stream, postponing decisions.

—*OCC*, 138

P

Pain

The unanimous testimony of the saints and the mystics, from St Paul onwards, makes it clear that at the highest level of spirituality suffering becomes something desirable, if only as making a contribution to that sum of expiation which the human race as a body owes for its size. That contribution, when made in union with the merits of Christ's Passion, is certainly acceptable to God.

−OCC, 334

The Crucified hangs there to answer the questionings of our intellect. What is the meaning, what is the value of pain? Why does man have to endure it? Or, granted that, why is its distribution among men so unequal, disproportionate to the merits of the souls affected by it? . . . in so far as our meditations deal faithfully, though in a humble and reverent spirit, with the doctrine of God made Man, sinless yet suffering for sins; in so far as we honestly propose to ourselves the questions we all know so well − Who hangs here? Doing what? By what means? At what moment of time? In what manner? For what purpose? . . . we shall come away from our meditation of the Passion both firmer in our faith and more reconciled to the pains and the sorrows that the sons of Adam are called upon to suffer − suffer them in such company as that.

−PAS, 176

Papacy

If the papacy be dead, then the Catholic Church is dead, and if the Catholic Church be dead, Christ has failed. Close down the churches. Shut up the Bible. Let us have no grinning death mask of Anglo-Catholicism to mock at our despair. But Peter is still there.

—UAS, 378

Parables

Our Lord's parables seem, now and again, more applicable to our own times than to his. Those labourers in the vineyard, quarrelling over their differentials, have a twentieth-century air, and there was nothing the dishonest steward did not know about commissions. But, above all, the guest who was swept into the marriage feast with all the other down-and-outs, only to be ejected in the end because he had no wedding-garment—how clearly Our Lord must have foreseen the prodigious importance we attach, nowadays, to clothes!

—LIG, 25

It would be quite natural to suppose that the Incarnate Revelation of Truth would announce a single message to all alike in plain, unmistakable language . . . as a matter of fact he did not, and has told us that he did not. After uttering the parable—surely a very simple one—of the sower sowing his seed, he goes out of his way to explain that he does not want all his audience to penetrate the full meaning of what he is talking about. That, surely, is something for us to think over.

—PAS, 75

Parishioners

What sort of influence is yours in the parish? Are you one of the whisperers; one of the tale-bearers who know all the scandal of the district? Are you one of those self-contained people who never find time to do anything for their neighbours. . . . Are you one of the murmurers who tell everybody how much better the parish was run in the old days? Are you anxious to discuss grievances. . . . Then the stones of this church will rise up in witness against you. . . . It is people like you that make [parish unity] crumble away.

—*OCC*, 363

It is possible to be too much of a parishioner. I mean, to have such an exaggerated sense of your own importance to the congregation that you are jealous of any infringement of your rights, even if you find somebody installed in what happens to be your favourite seat. Not a flower must be put on the altar, not a light turned off, not a hymnbook returned to its place, without your sanction. Oh, it is all infinitively small; but how cruelly these infinitely small things can disturb the peace of the parish!

—*OCC*, 370

Passing the Torch

Nearly everybody as years go on, [senses] it is time for us to be laid on the shelf: and, you know, we can make a lot of difference to the happiness and the quietness of the world, according as we determine to make ourselves unpleasant about it or determine to take it in St John the Baptist's spirit . . . the man who was the prophet of a nation at thirty years old, and died almost unknown, a mere historical memory, a year or so later.

—*UAS*, 349

Patriotism

Nationalism narrows our sympathies, patriotism broadens them—it extends our vision of neighbourliness beyond the parish pump. That it is a supernatural virtue, nobody pretends; it is a natural virtue which religion must needs canonise, like friendship. Like friendship, it does not excuse us from higher claims, such as those of justice. But in itself it enlarges us; it is the mother of heroisms.

—*LIG*, 104

Saint Paul

It would not be Saint Paul if he did not digress.

—*PAS*, 502

For him [the Church] is the bride of Christ; it is the building of which Christ is the corner stone; it is the body of which Christ is head.

—*PAS*, 514

Nothing less than paradox will content Saint Paul.

—*PAS*, 518

There is no "Futurism" about S. Paul: when he does look forward, it is with the hourly expectation of a thunder-clap.

—*SLS*, 113

Peace of Soul

For that, we need tranquillity, recollection; how are we to think about God or eternity, with daily needs and worldly preoccupations and public cares so weighing on our minds? The thought of God seems to get crowded out; our own sins get overlooked—they are so petty, compared with the needs of a distracted world, the perils of an uncertain future.

—*PAS*, 237

Peace Propaganda

In the years between 1918 and 1939 we overreached ourselves by our own idealism. We were so determined to banish war from the world that we refused to discuss . . . the proposals that were made for humanizing the methods of it. To have a convention against air attack upon undefended towns seemed almost blasphemous; it was like licensing brothels—you were parleying with the forbidden thing. Are we going to adopt the same policy again? Much propaganda has been made out of the atom on those familiar lines. This new engine of destruction, we are told, will make War *impossible* in future. Yet we were told the same, in the peace propaganda of the twenties, about the influence of poisonous gas on the future of warfare. And while we told one another, with wise shakings of the head, that poisonous gases had made war impossible in future, we were paving the way for the bloodiest war in all history, in the course of which neither side dropped a gas bomb.

—*GOD,* 73

Penance

The just persons who appear to have no need of penance are those who, to their own anxious peril, regard themselves as justified by their own merits . . . we shall meet it again in discussing the parable of the Pharisee and the Publican, and the conditions requisite for penance. It is Jew against Gentile, works against grace.

—*PAS,* 127

People (Modern)

Modern people are like little boys who have been to the conjurer, and come back and try and imitate him to their families, making the same sort of passes with their hands and producing eggs out of their pocket-handkerchiefs, only there is no trick in it and no magic at all. They have seen what is done, but they have not understood what is being done.

—*SAF,* 59

The Person

It's all nonsense, you complain, to talk about "person" and "nature" as if they were two quite separate things. . . . When you turn your thought inwards, and think about yourself, who is thinking about whom, or what is thinking about what? You are not simply thinking about your thought about yourself; because that would mean that you were thinking about your thought about your thought about your thought about yourself and so on *ad infinitum.* No, the term of your thought is *you,* the person who is thinking. And in doing so, you have already divided yourself up, in a sense, into two; the intellectual nature which is thinking, and the person, somehow mysteriously connected with that intellectual nature, who is being thought about. . . . [W]e've come up against yet another of those gaps in our thought, where the soil of natural mystery gives room for the flower of supernatural mystery to blossom. When our Lord thought about himself, the intellectual nature which thought was human; the Person who was being thought about was not human, but divine. That is mystery, if you like; but it is mystery in clear-cut terms.

—ISG, 143–44

The divine regard falls on everything singly. It is a weakness of our human minds that we must see things, and even people, in groups, in masses; we are not up to the strain of seeing them individually. . . . That is why, if you believe in the doctrine of Providence at all, you have got to believe in a Providence which looks after us individually. . . . We (except perhaps when we are in love) find it difficult to think about our fellow creatures except in a general way; masses of men, movements, and tendencies in history. . . . But to God, each of us is unique, and each of us is the one that matters.

—OCC, 264

Our Lord tells us that no sparrow falls to the ground without our heavenly Father's will; every hair of our heads, he says, is numbered. That picture of an omnipotence which takes every detail into account is something which baffles the imagination; but we can't doubt that every individual life, if we only knew it, is worked out on a pattern, and it will be the best pattern for us if we will only correspond with it; God does underwrite the business of our souls.

—OCC, 335

God does not use his human creatures as his instruments, but as his fellow-agents. That is the Calvinist's mistake, to suppose that grace overpowers the soul upon which it is conferred, so that no choice and no liberty and no merit can remain.

—UAS, 321

Personality

The influence of a personality may take the form of a great love. Probably it does take that form more often than we think; we are all inclined to be a little cynical and disrespectful in our attitude to other people's love affairs. There are really people who find life worth living because they are allowed, often with very little in the way of recognition or return, to serve and to reverence a woman they love. . . . All this demands faith; for your estimate of the personality which means so much to you is not a thing which can be tested or proved by any form of demonstration; you believe in the person who so dominates your life, and it is the very fact that your belief in him has an element of uncertainty in it that makes the whole thing worth while. A person might play you false, might prove unworthy of your admiration; it is precisely that "might" which makes the thing worth while. It is because you are uncertain that it is possible for you to have faith; and with that faith happiness comes into your life, and you find a new attitude towards the world.

—*ISG*, 102

Person (Sanctity of)

You pass through the streets as you go to your daily work, and see all those thousands of your fellow beings—faces hardened by money-getting, faces impudent with the affectation of vice, faces vacant with frivolity, faces lined with despair—and it seems to you impossible that each one of these faces, with so little recognition in it of a divine vocation or of eternal destiny, can yet represent a soul for which God cares. And yet he does care, if theology is to mean anything; cares for this one as he . . . cared for the penitent thief.

—*PAS*, 303

There are two really staggering affirmations which the Christian religion involves, compared with which all its other doctrines are easy to assimilate. One is this: God cares for everybody. And the other is this: God cares for me.

—*PAS*, 303

Pharisees

It is always the Pharisees and lawyers that our Lord singles out as typical of that pride and blindness which preaches what it dares not to practice.

—*PAS*, 82

Philosophers (Modern)

In our time, if you ask, in the popular phrase, "Where do we go from here?", the sages of the world have no answer. They have boxed the compass, from a mood of exaggerated hopes into a mood of exaggerated despairs. But for us, there are no such changes of mood. The thing we live by today is the thing we lived by a hundred years ago. The world's glory passes, the Catholic faith remains.

—OCC, 261

Today, when the world has become so fuddled with its own philosophies that men cannot be sure whether two and two really make four, whether black is not really white under another aspect, they all agree on one thing—that the Catholic religion can't be true. They will tell you one moment that it is impossible to discover whether truth exists, and the next moment that the Catholic religion is certainly false—such is their logic. The Catholic religion must obviously be a deception, because it claims to know what is true.

—PAS, 183

Philosophy (Modern)

To befit such an age, a philosopher must be one who studies, not the thing known, but the mind that knows it. Descartes neglected the metaphysical approach because he was lost in contemplating the greatness of the human mind, just as Pascal neglected it because he was lost in contemplating the miseries of the human soul.

—GOD, 28

Physics and Chemistry

It is not true that modern physics, or modern chemistry, or that liaison between chemistry and physics which has been so much under discussion lately, have superseded the whole "world-background" against which the theology of the Christian religion was built up, and antiquated the one with the other. . . . But metaphysical thought does not depend on this or that physical theory; and, if the study of metaphysics is in these latter days unpopular, that is because the science has been neglected, not because it

156

has been exploded. It seems quite possible that the hesitations of the modern physicist over the very nature of the subject with which he is dealing may lead to a revived interest in metaphysics; if so, theology will not be the loser. Meanwhile, it would no doubt be dangerous for the Christian apologist to base his arguments on gaps in the physical theory, and he is not likely to do so.

—BCM, 271–72

Piety (Christian)

There is this curious paradox running through the whole history of Christian piety—that holy people have always despised the intellect, and yet they have been the greatest educators of the world.

—UAS, 912

Pipes

A pipe that refuses to draw just after breakfast is guilty of desertion in the face of the enemy.

—SAF, 34

Pius X

If I meant that holy communion is a privilege reserved ... for an *élite* of almost perfect souls, then I should be falling back into the error of the Jansenists, and I should be wronging the memory of that great Pope who has just been raised to the altars of the Church. For whatever else St Pius the Tenth is remembered, he will be remembered for having thrown open the gates of the sanctuary to hesitating and struggling souls; to the unworthy who know themselves to be unworthy.

—PAS, 273–74

Plato

We remember ... things he said about the immortality of the soul, and the purgations and punishments that awaited it in a future life.... And it makes us recall other things Plato wrote; about the just man who would be scourged and go to the stake because the men of his day didn't understand what real justice meant; and about the true shepherd, not the one who is out to make money. And that sets us thinking about all the other odd anticipations of Christian ideas which you find in the pagan world.

—OCC, 344

Politicians

A little Baby in a manger, a hunted criminal, a malefactor weighted with the instrument of his own punishment—so our Lord looked to the world; not otherwise did his Church look—does his Church look, to the scornful eye of the politicians that reject it. Christianity was the religion of slaves; it has abolished slavery. It was thrown to the lions in the amphitheatre; it has abolished the amphitheatre. Absolute monarchy, like a flustered giant, laboured to crush it; it has outlived absolute monarchy. Silently through the centuries the supernatural miracle has worked, like nature's miracle of fermentation.

—PAS, 90

Politicians (Modern)

[Today] we are inclined to look askance at Divine "punishments", because modern legislators, more than their predecessors, are influenced by a humanitarianism which is anxious rather to see that order is kept, than to ensure that Justice is done.

—SLS, 4

The Poor

Some few of us are called to a life of holy poverty; all of us are called to a life of detachment. And in order to achieve that detachment from worldly goods which belongs to our Christian profession, we must learn to realize the true scale of values. We are poor, we Catholics; it is easy for people to keep out of our way and pretend that they do not see us.

—PAS, 194

It's often the poor despised souls, the Samaritans of the race, that give most thanks for the blessings which others would think almost contemptible.

—*UAS*, 374

The Pope

The Pope's intentions, how lightly those words fall on the ear. . . . Have you ever thought what it would be like to be the Holy Father, to take, for a single day, for a single hour, the strain of his world-wide office? When you pray for the Pope's intentions at Mass, take your stand beside him in imagination, the man on whom we Christians, millions of us, have laid the burden of our common solicitudes.

—*PAS*, 265

Positive Outlook

However depressing the state of the world is, we Christians are meant to watch in the positive sense; we are meant to tidy things up, as well as they can be tidied up, against the day of our Lord's return. Like servants waiting for their master's home-coming; not anticipating it with alarm, and deciding that it will be safer not to have a dance in the drawing-room for fear he should come back in the middle—no, looking forward to it; running out on to the drive to see if they can catch the sound of carriage-wheels. And, in the intervals of that, doing a hundred little odd jobs against time; a room to be dusted, a floor to be polished, a fire to be made up, so that the house shall look a hundred per cent comfortable when he steps inside.

—*LIG*, 121–22

Poverty (Apostolic)

If the Church Christ founded had come to an end, when did it come to an end? The rage for apostolic poverty prompted the convenient answer: 'In the fourth century, when the Donation of Western Europe by Constantine to St. Sylvester made the Church a property-owning body.' The Spiritual Franciscans . . . fell back on the belief that the Church had unchurched herself when she turned her back on poverty, exactly as the Donatists,

159

all those centuries earlier, believed she had unchurched herself by turning her back on martyrdom.

—EN, III

Praise

How much of what the world praises, of what the world finds attractive in you, is to be put down, when you judge the matter calmly and soberly, to three imperfect or even sinful motives—vainglory, worldly respect, respect of persons?

—PAS, 468

Prayer

What we mean, in the last resort, by "an answer to prayer", is that from the beginning of time, before he set about the building of the worlds, God foreknew every prayer that human lips would breathe, and took it into account. That, and nothing less, is the staggering claim which we make every time we say the "Our Father".

—CAL, 94

Mental prayer is prayer without words; contemplative prayer (at least in its initial stage) is prayer without images; if the phrase may be allowed, we do not think about God, we think God.

—EN, 251

When you and I talk about the presence of God, we are talking about our prayers. We are wondering whether there isn't some way of making ourselves realize, when we are on our knees, the fact, which we know perfectly well for a fact, namely that God is there. If we could only realize that, we tell ourselves, our prayer would be less disappointing to us, and perhaps to him.

—LAY, 46

God not only (fore)sees all the events which (will) happen, but also (fore)sees all the prayers which human beings (will) offer. There should be no difficulty, then, about his taking into consideration all the prayers of mankind at the same moment in which he determines the whole fortunes of mankind ... you must think of him as taking into account all human petitions, and allowing them to have some weight (we don't know how much) in the ordering of his Providence.

—OR, 23

The French peasant who was asked what was going on when he sat praying before the tabernacle, and replied, "I look at him, and he looks at me", had evidently got the secret of it. A mere clinging of the soul to God, to a God not represented to the mind by images, but veiled in a darkness which is yet luminous to the eye of faith; without any multiplicity of acts, so that one mystic was able to declare she never said anything in her prayer except the word "Yes"—that is prayer, and prayer of a very high order; perhaps of the highest order.

—PAS, 481

Praying

Do you pray with your eyes shut, or open? The difference is not a mere difference of tradition, or a mere nervous trick; it is a symbol. . . . When you pray with your eyes shut you are, in effect, saying something like this: "My God, I am very grateful to you for all your creatures, but they are a terrible distraction to me. So I am going to make a gesture by keeping my eyes shut; that gate, at least, shall be barred against distraction." And when you pray with your eyes open, you are saying something like this: "My God, I know that you have ordained your creatures to lead me to you. Let me read you in them, just as I can look at black ink-marks on a page, and read in them without effort the thought of the writer who committed them to paper."

—LIG, 131

Prejudice

[Prejudice] is a soil which is deliberately hardened . . . a sort of macadamization of the conscience.

—UAS, 333

The Press

Men, after all, are children, and the Press is a kind of governess that must first (for the sake of peace) find out what game the children want to play, and then (for the sake of discipline) appear to have been the originator of the suggestion.

—CAL, 9

The Press does not actually mould opinion, but it hardens the mould into which opinion is already setting, and exaggerates, to some extent, the contours which it is destined to take.

—CAL, 10

Pride

That spirit of pride, which is the enemy of all holiness.

—OCC, 74

Are there grudges which could be forgone, if pride did not keep whispering in your ear, "No, one cannot forgive a thing like that"? Is there some estrangement between you and a kinsman or a friend which began (you know it) with a fault of yours, which might yet be healed on both sides if you would only admit it was you who were in the wrong? "The kindness of God our Saviour dawned on us"—he came so far to meet us, and we, to imitate his kindness, have such a little way to go.

—OCC, 290

Next to thinking that you can do without God the most dangerous mistake you can make is thinking that God cannot do without you.

—PAS, 121

The Priesthood and Dangerous Instincts

[There are the] instincts of self-preservation, of self-assertion, of self-reproduction. If you let them get out of control, the first leads to avarice, the second to pride, the third to immodesty. The three vows of holy religion are designed to be their direct antidotes; the vow of poverty curbs the instinct of self-preservation, the vow of obedience, that of self-assertion, the vow of chastity, that of self-reproduction. Our state of life pledges us to a higher standard in these matters than is observed by the laity. And because we are pledged to a high standard, nature will always be trying to get her own back. We can't make much of a calf, and therefore we are tempted to make the best calf we can.

—*RFP*, 69–70

Priests

You must pray for your priests. The spirit of a great institute like the Benedictine congregation does not survive automatically through the centuries; there is always danger, as time goes on, that such an institute, depending for its life not so much on any principles of organization as upon the influence of a subtle spirit which animates it, will lose the freshness and the purity of its character.

—*OCC*, 18–19

There is one moment during the Mass, just about the *Domine non sum dignus,* when the priest, if he is not careful, catches sight of his own features reflected in the paten . . . at that sacred moment, an alien thing intrudes upon his thoughts, the sight of his own features . . . it is the kind of distraction he can make good use of. Because he will do well to consider the contrast between what he sees on the paten, and what he meant (and was meant) to see there. He looked there to catch sight of a sinless Victim; he caught sight, instead, of a sinful priest. *Domine, non sum dignus* — how can *this* be worthy to receive *that?*

—*PAS*, 330

Perhaps it would be a good thing if every Christian, certainly if every priest, could dream once in his life that he were Pope, and wake from that nightmare in a sweat of agony.

—*UAS*, 430

163

Priests and the Church

All that we probably shan't hear about ourselves. But we shall hear very much that sort of thing said about the Church we love more than life. That our claims are built on falsehood; that we are an insignificant force in the world to-day; that we are dying out, or at least have lost so much prestige that we shall never recover from it; that we are kill-joys, preaching a medieval morality to a world which has grown out of it; that . . . we Catholics, what we do isn't worth reporting, what we say isn't worth repeating. All that we shall hear said, or read it in books and newspaper articles by people who don't like us. But none of it matters; none of it matters a bit, as long as *we* haven't been responsible, for giving a bad impression of the ministry we exercise; as long as *we*, Christ's ambassadors, have done our best to do what nobody can ever really do—represent him.

—*PL,* 34–35

Printing Presses

On the whole it is true that printing is the antithesis of gunpowder, and operates more effectually in assassination than in massacre. Dynamite is kept under lock and key more easily than ideas. You can control the printing press, at least in its early stages, without much physical difficulty; though even here it is well to remember that Campion found it easier to print his *Ten Reasons* under the eaves of Stonor Court unobserved than Fawkes to store up his barrels. But censorship is a cumbrous and an odious work; nor can human calculation ever make certain which ideas are live wires and which are duds.

—*BCM,* 4–5

Progress

We may strut and give ourselves airs, and tell one another that we have conquered practically the whole of nature and it is only a matter of time before we conquer the rest of it; but the fact remains, we were made of the slime of the earth; dust thou art, as the priest says to us on Ash Wednesday, dust thou art, and to dust shalt thou return. If we are anything more than dust, it is only because God saw fit, of his free bounty, to do something else.

—*OCC,* 226

Sudden new departures, these much-advertised attempts to break with the past— do they really break with the past, or are they not a revival of the past in modern dress? Vanity of vanities, saith the preacher; there is no new thing under the sun.

—PAS, 394

Two hundred years ago thieves were hanged: two hundred years hence a murderer will get six months—I call that going back behind Cain. Three hundred years ago we burned witches: three hundred years hence we shall all be spiritualists—I call that going back to the devil.

—SAF, 113

Prophets

There is the double tragedy of the prophet; he must speak out, so that he makes men dislike him, and he must be content to believe that he is making no impression whatever.

—OCC, 411

Prophets (Modern)

Actually, of course, it matters very little to the prophets of the modern age whether we others are happy or not. For we have embarked on a hundred-year plan, and we are being invited to make the sacrifice of all we found pleasant and all we held sacred in the hope that, possibly, our great-nephews will be thankful to us.

—BCM, 95

Propriety

People do manage to keep straight just because there is a strong moral tone in the society around them—a moral tone which makes itself felt in a variety of social conventions. And the danger, of course, is that they should confuse propriety with morality. The danger is that in taking the laws of morality and the conventions of propriety equally for granted, they should assume that the

165

two things stand or fall together. And then, if the proprieties go, the moral principles—for such people—will go too.

—UAS, 129

Proselytizing

Indiscriminate attempts to convert other people mean, at the best, that you give people a dislike for Catholicism; at the worst, that you shake what faith they have in Christianity altogether, so that the last state of them is worse than the first. No, your duty is to defend the faith to the best of your power where you can see it is being misrepresented.

—UAS, 84

Protestantism

Protestantism, in revolt against the Petrine claims, and basing its most characteristic theology on a false reading of St Paul's epistle to the Romans, could hardly fail to draw invidious comparisons, in which St Paul always came out best.

—OCC, 3

It's Protestantism which decries reason, and tells you that your act of faith in God must be a pure act of the will, without argument or motive. Catholic doctrine doesn't want you to take anything on faith until you're intellectually convinced that (for example) the Resurrection was a historical fact.

—SAF, 179

Protestants

They appealed . . . to the Bible—the Bible interpreted by scholarship; that is, by their own scholarship. To the enthusiast, the Bible is infallible when interpreted by an inspired person. To the Reformers, it possessed an inherent infallibility, and needed only clarification, which was a matter for the learned.

—EN, 133–34

What is it exactly that the old-fashioned Protestant misses as he kneels at the communion-rails? To be sure, he finds there nothing of the miraculous; he has lost sight of what is our chief motive for admiration and gratitude; if the doctrine of transubstantiation is proposed to him, he dismisses it at once as a piece of medieval superstition. . . . His devotional life is impoverished, rather, for *this* reason—that his communion service has nothing of Mass about it.

—*PAS*, 254–55

[I]t is quite certain that there are no Protestants in the world under the age of five.

—*UAS*, 80

There are very few Protestants who are Protestants in bad faith. They are in good faith, so long as they remain outside the Church through invincible ignorance.

—*UAS*, 81

They only think of us [Catholics] as people who are suffering from an incurable and disfiguring and unfortunately contagious disease.

—*UAS*, 354

Providence

God does not disclose his design beforehand; we shall see the plans in heaven. But it is all *meant;* there was never yet a slip of the Craftsman's fingers; your niche is there, waiting for you, if you will allow hammer and chisel to do their work.

—*OCC*, 295

Psychology (Modern)

If psychology should succeed in throwing doubt on *all* our mental processes, it would *ipso facto* throw doubt on its own, and fall into the intellectual suicide which is the inevitable fate of dogmatic scepticism.

—*BCM*, 28

If patriotism, ambition, moral indignation, the love of natural beauty, etc., can be shown to be misinterpreted echoes from the consciousness of childhood, based in the last resort on sexual perversion or wounds in the tender centres of our nervous system, then indeed we shall have gone far towards unifying our experience. True, existence itself may take on less dazzling colours when we have learned thus to re-read our values. But that will be the sacrifice made, as sacrifices must ever be made, on the altar of Truth—if indeed Truth itself has not by that time been reduced to a neurosis with the rest of them.

—BCM, 45

It is one of the chief drawbacks about the new psychology that it cannot establish its unit; cannot decide where the line comes between the normal and the abnormal. This makes it a weapon all the more handy for the popular philosopher; he can bandy names without the responsibility of deciding for himself or for his readers whether the states to which he is referring are pathological or not.

—BCM, 100

Publicans and Pharisees

[The publican] simply goes on beating his breast, bowing towards the earth, and repeating "God be merciful to me a sinner". And yet he goes to his house justified rather than the Pharisee—and all because of an attitude of mind. The one is good and knows it, the other is bad and knows it; and it is not what they are that makes the difference, but their knowledge of what they are.

—PAS, 129

Public Grievances

How they fill us with embarrassment, our fellow-Christians who are always getting worked up over things we take calmly! "It's a scandal", they say; "some protest must be made about it".... Let us admit that we are some- times in the right; to be always up in arms over trifles is to lessen the rarity-value of your protests; the modern public has grown distrustful of "pressure-groups."

And yet, how we despise in others the cynicism or the flabbiness which simply "can't be bothered" in a world so fertile of abuses! At least let us beware, as age creeps on, of a certain moral hardening which familiarity with the world is apt to breed in us. Let us not despise altogether the weakness in which God's strength is made perfect.

—*LIG*, 28

Pulpits

It is a bad habit in historians to take at their face value the hysterical exaggerations of the pulpit.

—*EN*, 396

Purgatory

Because we don't know that a particular soul is in heaven yet, we behave as if it wasn't; and if we think of heaven we think of it as peopled only by the canonized saints—is purgatory really such a long business? Oughtn't we to think of heaven as peopled already by millions and millions of redeemed souls, uncanonized and unheard of, Tom, Dick and Harry, ransomed by the blood of Jesus Christ?

—*OCC*, 318

Pursuits (Scholarly)

But all these desirable aims, if you see them against the background of a single human life, are only toys after all, only extras; they are not, taken alone, worth living for. The scholar who lives only for his subject is but the fragment of a man; he lives in a shadow-world, mistaking means for ends.

—*OCC*, 256–57

Q

Quakerism

Quakerism, from the first, had no sympathy with coercion. But it did not tolerate; agitation, of its very nature, is intolerant.

—EN, 146

Quakerism's "Inner Light"

The truth is that if you adopt the inner light as your rule of faith, it necessarily supersedes and (if need be) overrides the authority of Scripture.

—EN, 152

To live by the inner light is in some sense to be divinized, to *realize* the dwelling of God's Spirit in us; and a theology untrammelled by the traditions of orthodox Christianity will naturally interpret this as meaning that sin has become impossible to us.

—EN, 153

Quietism

It is a vulgar error, based on a mere verbal confusion, to suppose that Quietism consists in leading a quiet life.... Curiously, the chief complaint made against the Quietists by their adversaries was that they would not keep quiet.

—*EN*, 261–62

Quotations

There is danger ... in quotations.

—*EN*, 455

R

Rationalist

He is prejudiced against the proofs of revelation we are going to offer him. . . . We shall find him telling us, for example, that he doesn't believe in miracles. But, if he would make his thought coherent, he would find that he really draws the line at divine interference of any kind . . . it is the divine intrusion he would resent. If a dog got up and made a public speech in the middle of Carfax, it would worry him, but he wouldn't really *mind*, as long as the dog kept off theological topics.

—HS, 51–52

Reality

Always, it is the things which affect us outwardly and impress themselves on our senses that are the shams, the imaginaries; reality belongs to the things of the spirit.

—PAS, 258

Reason

If, then, in making terms with the other Christianities, you renounce altogether the intellectual approach, you have cut the ground under your feet. You have broken down the barriers between Christian and Christian, only to break down the bridges between Christians and those outside. St Thomas could reason with Avicenna; Marcel cannot reason with Sartre.

—OCC, 356

Reason and Revelation

Our mental powers also are from God; to write these off as hopelessly corrupted by the Fall is an extravagance quite unwarranted by the Christian tradition. To live by, and for, a series of supposedly Divine communications is, too commonly, to cultivate an unhealthy state of mind, avid of portents and ill protected from the inroads of superstition.

—EN, 587

What the Church insists on is this, that it is theoretically possible for any human being, even at a low stage of development, to find out God for himself if he will use the natural gift of reason which God has given him . . . and we cannot but believe that God will judge, in such cases, with a mercy proportionate to the lack of opportunity. But you mustn't say that the knowledge of God's existence can *only* come to us through a revelation, public or private; that there is no other way in which such an idea could ever have been entertained; that is heresy.

—UAS, 22

The Reformation

Nothing is more characteristic of the Reformation period than the outbreak of amateur theologies which was occasioned by the disintegration of religion in Europe. Any tinker or weaver thought that, if he had the Bible open before him, he had as good a right to construct a theology out of it for himself as to accept a theology at second hand from a recognized preacher.

—CAL, 5

The whole Reformation movement was the apotheosis of the learned clerk; you might not read *your* Bible, you must read Luther's Bible.

—EN, 115

Reformers

On the whole your non-religious man is a more successful reformer, because he can work for the future without worrying over the souls of the people who are on the streets here and now.

—DIF, 27

Rejoicing

"Jesus rejoiced"—that, surely, is the most astonishing proof of his full humanity. He, who in his divine nature could suffer no diminution of his eternal blessedness . . . condescended nevertheless to feel and to be refreshed by a human sentiment of joy. In that hour Jesus rejoiced in the spirit, and said, "I thank thee, O Father, Lord of heaven and earth, because thou hast hidden these things from the wise and prudent, and hast revealed them to little ones". . . . [1] He rejoices, not because everybody is prepared to receive his message; no, some will reject, will persecute, will crucify him. No, he rejoices because the right people will receive his message, the simple, the child-like, the humble.

—PAS, 189

Relativism

We have all got so accustomed to a mental atmosphere in which everything is graded; one thing differs from another in degree, rather than in kind. There is no absolute standard about our human criticisms, no black and white, only shades of grey. . . . [But] there is one nasty bump waiting for all of us, death; there are no shades or gradations about that.

—HS, 169

Relativity

I do not think any of us will live long without finding that "Relativity" has become as much a catch-word in the theological debates of our own time as "Evolution" was in the time of our grandfathers.

—BCM, 187

[1]Lk 10:21.

Relativity; bred in a culture of terms we could not understand, and calculations we could not follow. Hitherto, although we were robbed of Aristotle, Euclid had been left us; now, even the basic certitudes of the mind, certitudes which even Kant had tolerated in the mind, as long as they did not seek to go outside it, were hauled up for revision. I have never heard an exponent of Relativity deny the principle that "things which are equal to the same thing are equal to one another", but none of us would be surprised at being told that "it only holds good on a certain level." And relativity threatened to be a form of mind-conditioning even more relentless than evolution. Evolution in morals was bad enough; where should we be when it came to relativity in morals? The stars in their courses were fighting against us, if we could still believe that they had any.

—GOD, 32

Religion

Lenin condemned religion as the opium of the people; Mr Wells is prepared to tolerate it, under proper safeguards, as a kind of cocktail for the reformer.

—BCM, 226

Religion is, by its derivation, something that ties a man down, restrains him. Whether it be true or false, it is an influence which prevents a man from behaving in a way in which he might otherwise have behaved, and does so in the name of some higher power with whose authority he dare not palter. The idea is most easily grasped if you confine your attention to the taking of oaths.

—CAL, 37

Religion, in fact, if it is to keep the sense of its derivation, is not something which I have got hold of, but something which has got hold of me.

—CAL, 39

The chief mission and the chief difficulty of the Jewish prophets was to persuade their fellow-countrymen that it wasn't much good trying to appease God with the blood of bulls and goats if you went on bearing false witness and oppressing the poor. . . . Religion wasn't meant to tie you down from touching a dead body or seething a kid in its mother's milk. It was meant to tie

175

you down to a rule of right living, a rule of love towards God and towards your fellow man.

—HS, 3–4

I think the most interesting answer to the question, "What difference does religion make?" is just to point at the people who haven't got any, and leave it to be solved by inspection.

—HS, 7

"Religion" under the Christian dispensation has changed its meaning. It does not stand for a mere attitude, it stands for a transaction . . . for the paying off of a debt. Religion . . . means the offering up of a man's self to God; for us Christians, it means the offering up to God of Jesus Christ, the perfect Victim once for all immolated in our stead, and of ourselves in union with that sacrifice.

—HS, 8

Religion (Comparative)

Our Lord's claim is not just to satisfy this or that need of common life, meet this or that situation in common life. He offers to give us a new, supernatural life, complete with all its faculties, in the midst of this troubled and precarious world. No one else offers us that; no one else dares claim of us the faith which will enable us to believe in that. Reject him if you will, but do not try to match him with the world's other teachers.

—HS, 114

Religion (Modern)

Since we took to inventing our own religion for ourselves, instead of accepting the authority of the Church, we have lost all sense of supernatural sanction behind our ideas of right and wrong. Each nation and each citizen has a private philosophy and a private code. That's the trouble. And when you've invented the code or the philosophy for yourself, you suddenly find at some moment of emergency that it doesn't bind you. How could it? The stream doesn't rise higher than the source.

—SAF, 101

Religion (Victorian)

What undermined the religion of the Victorians was not so much that Evolution had emptied heaven for them, as that Evolution had destroyed their confidence in their own individual value; with Nature crying out that a thousand types had gone, was it possible to believe that a single soul, though it were Lord Byron, though it were General Gordon, awoke the Divine interest?

—GOD, 55

Religiosity (Modern)

Modern religiosity is not incompatible with an increase in the proportion of registry-office marriages, or with a series of Sunday mornings spent on the roads and on the golf-links.

—CAL, 1

There is no evidence that people are more religious; there *is* evidence that people are fonder of talking about religion, and of talking about it in public.

—CAL, 2–3

Religious

Almost every great religious genius has felt, at some time in his life, many a great religious genius has felt at the very close of his life, the sense of failure—he has laboured in vain, spent his strength without cause.

—OCC, 236

Revelation

It would be rather bad luck on the human race if there hadn't been a revelation, considering what a poor show we should have put up if we had been left to construct a religion for ourselves. When I use the term "bad luck", I am not speaking theological language. One doesn't claim that God was *bound* to reveal himself; only that we should have expected him to reveal himself, considering how good he is.

—HS, 51

177

In the New Testament *progressive revelation* of the truth from God to the human soul, the context always makes it clear that the means by which this progress is to be attained is not philosophical discussion or critical investigation, but the spiritual vision which is attained only in mental prayer.

— *SLS*, 228

Rogues

I'm afraid it's perfectly true, and more true than most people realize, that a good many of the world's rogues are Catholics. It's extraordinary how often you will come across Catholic names when you are reading in the newspaper the records of crime, whether on a small scale or on a large scale. . . . Now, it's perfectly true that in a way this unholiness of Catholics is a compliment to our religion. Because it does mean that a Catholic does not necessarily cease to be a Catholic because he is a rogue. He knows what is right even when he is doing what is wrong. The Protestant as a rule will give up his faith first and his morals afterwards; with Catholics it is the other way round. The Protestant only feels his religion to be true as long as he goes on practising it; the Catholic feels the truth of his religion as something independent of himself, which does not cease to be valid when he, personally, fails to live up to its precepts.

— *ISG*, 87

Romance

Ordinary romance was invented, one would think, by a wearied historian, who, finding himself, like most historians, unable to give a true account of the past, and willing, unlike most historians, to confess his inability, sat down to write a kind of literature in which all his characters behaved exactly as he wanted them to, because they had no existence outside his own brain.

— *LIT*, 184

Rome

Rome stands altogether by itself; for Rome has the tradition of that apostle who was commanded to "confirm his brethren". Its Bishop has a tradition of doctrine which is, by divine guarantee, immune from error as is the general tradition of doctrine collectively given to the Church. Hence when heresies begin to arise, the attitude of the Roman Bishop is all-important.

—DIF, 126

The Rosary

The reason why we get tired of saying the rosary so much, is because we think about it so little. We don't treat it exactly as if it were a prayer-wheel, but we treat it very much as if it were a prayer-wheel; we don't really want to say it, we want to get it said. And of course that can't be the right way to go about it.

—LAY, 89

S

Sacraments

A person who tries to live a life that's pleasing to God without any sacraments to help him is always in danger of measuring everything by his own effort, and becoming rather smug and priggish about his own effort. But the sacramental system, whatever else it does, ought to teach us humility.

—HS, 182

Define the word "sacrament" how you will, the root idea of it is clearly this, that something purely spiritual and something purely physical are presented close side by side. And in human marriage . . . that dual character hits you in the face. Love, which is the most spiritual thing given in our experience outside of religion, is there side by side with the satisfaction of the purely physical.

—HS, 194–95

There is always life still as long as you do not abandon the sacraments.

—UAS, 323

The Sacred Heart

The Sacred Heart is the treasury of *all* those splendid qualities with which a perfect life was lived; is the repository of *all* those noble thoughts which mankind still venerate in the gospels. It was the Sacred Heart that burned with anger when the traders were driven out of the temple . . . it was the Sacred Heart that defied Pilate in his own judgment-hall. It is strong and stern and enduring; it hates prevarications and pretences. The perfect flowering of a human life, not on this occasion or that, but all through, all the time, the utter sacrifice of a human will—*that* is what the Sacred Heart means, and there is no picture, no statue on earth that can portray its infinite beauty.

—PAS, 423

Saints

We know that the saints, built, surely, in a different mould from ourselves, have desired, have prayed for, martyrdom; we know that suffering, for them, was not a nightmare to be avoided, but a privilege to be sued for, almost a right to be claimed.

—LAY, 179

The instinct of all Catholic Saints and philanthropists is to make the best of existing conditions, relieving the sufferings of the present and leaving the conditions to alter themselves.

—LIT, 27

When you try to make a saint accept a bishopric, it is like trying to make a child take medicine: the result is a perfect fury of dissent.

—OCC, 31

The philosopher blinks because he has come out of the darkness of his study into the light of common things; the saint blinks because he has come out of the light of his oratory into the darkness of the world. He has been with God; and in seeing, as we do not see, the greatness of God, he has seen, as we do not see, his own smallness.

—OCC, 32

The saint who has been with God, who has familiarized himself with the thought of God's greatness . . . what must he think when he comes back to the unreal pomps, the sordid competition, the pretentious would-be wisdom of the world's citizens? Must not he see man as a coxcomb, strutting about in borrowed plumes, and making himself ridiculous afresh with every fresh air he puts on of . . . self-assertion? Must not he see the world's mad competition as a fond striving for prizes not worth the dust of conflict, and only capable of deluding us because we never rest satisfied with their attainment, but press on at once after others no less transitory?

—*OCC*, 69

He has learned, somehow, to measure things by the standard of eternity, and the peace of his own soul really does mean more to him than the peace of his country. He deliberately breaks up our home, our comfortable home, the world.

—*OCC*, 111

The attitude of our non-Catholic friends towards the Catholic saints; they always contrive to discredit, in one of two ways, their witness to the faith. Either they will say: "This was a very unpleasant, narrow-minded man, of ridiculous personal habits; and if that is what saints are like we would sooner hear no more of them", or they will say: "Yes, this man was indeed a saint; but then he was not really a Roman Catholic. He was just a good Christian, as I and my wife are; he only happened to be in communion with the Pope because everybody was in those days."

—*OCC*, 115–16

"Some people", [Thomas à Kempis] complains, "feel drawn towards this saint or that with a kind of competitive love; and all the while the motive which influences them is human, not divine." The saints are the lights of the world, but the light which shines in them is borrowed.

—*OCC*, 154

What refreshment it is when we can turn from the contemplation of our own characters, with their imperfect motives, their confused issues, their vanities and their pettinesses, to the sight of a man who goes through the world with one single ambition, to promote the glory of God. There may be foibles and mannerisms about such a life, but they will be all on the surface; directly you ask yourself, "What is this man getting at?" you are forced to reply, "He is out for the greater glory of God, nothing else."

—PAS, 468

Salvation

If you think of our Lord in Gethsemane as a man not certain what is going to happen to him, and anxious to avoid death if he possibly can, you have a very commonplace situation, the Hero of which is not half so worth our admiration or imitation as Socrates. But if you think of our Lord as knowing that his best friend is to betray him, that his own people are going to put him to death, yet longing for the reversal of what he knows to be inevitable—then you get some picture, translated into human terms, of how God wills the salvation of all men, although he foresees that some will refuse his gift.

—DIF, 99

Sanctity

Sanctity is not a work done, it is a life lived.

—OCC, 53

Sanctity, St Philip used to say, rests within the compass of three inches; and he would point to his forehead to show that what he meant was the mortification of the *razionale*, the proper pride that is perfection's most fatal enemy.

—OCC, 74

Sanity

The true sanity realizes that the truth, let it be what it may, matters furiously.

—LIT, 163

Satan

To-day, whatever we may believe about God working miracles, it is exceedingly difficult to believe that Satan, or someone very like him, is not working miracles to the undoing of souls.

—SLS, 65

Satire

It is born to scourge the persistent and ever-recurrent follies of the human creature as such. And, for anybody who has the humility to realize that it is aimed at him, and not merely at his neighbours, satire has an intensely remedial effect; it purifies the spiritual system of man as nothing else that is human can possibly do.

—ESS, 36

Satire vs. Humor

The humorist runs with the hare; the satirist hunts with the hounds.

—ESS, 31

Satirist vs. Prophet

There is a melancholy difference between the fate of the prophet and that of his disreputable brother, the satirist. For the prophet, though his fortunes be ruined and his world crashes about him, has at least the gloomy satisfaction of muttering, "I told you so." But the satirist, who also told them so, refuses to be comforted; not only are his worst dreams realized, but they have ceased to have value as satire; there is no escape for him, except the disingenuous pretence that he really meant it.

—BCM, 39

Scandal

A scandal [carries] further than a tale of sanctity; our Blessed Lady lived and died unknown, but all Jerusalem knew when Judas hanged himself.

—*PAS,* 100

Schism and Nationalism

In a word, nationalism plays its part in the history of Donatism, but for the most part as an unconscious undercurrent. Such undercurrents are by no means rare in theological controversy; who shall say whether the Scots disliked the Book of Common Prayer because it was Episcopalian, or because it was English?

—*EN,* 63

Schisms

The pattern is always repeating itself, not in outline merely but in detail. Almost always the enthusiastic movement is denounced as an innovation, yet claims to be preserving, or to be restoring, the primitive discipline of the Church.

since Vat II yes!!

—*EN,* 1

Schism begets schism; once the instinct of discipline is lost, the movement breeds rival prophets and rival coteries, at the peril of its internal unity. Always the first fervours evaporate; prophecy dies out, and the charismatic is merged in the institutional. 'The high that proved too high, the heroic for earth too hard'—it is a fugal melody that runs through the centuries.

—*EN,* 1

The enthusiast always begins by trying to form a church within the Church, always ends by finding himself committed to sectarian opposition.

—*EN,* 109

[The] belief . . . of all enthusiasts, was that it did not matter who had founded your particular religious group, or when. What mattered was that you should follow Christ; if you did that, you were *ipso facto* inside the only Church that counted.

—*EN*, 112–13

Scholarship

The pursuit of learning, if it goes unchecked, can lead to a kind of idolatry. Historical truth, scientific truth, the method of philosophy, that delicate balance of the mind which we call scholarship, are in themselves values which can claim our reverence . . . although in fact the light which shines from them is not theirs; God is their Sun, and it is from him their radiance is borrowed.

—*OCC*, 256

Scholarship (Modern)

This tyranny of the hypothesis over the mind of the scholar, which is a matter of psychology, not a thing that can be brought home to him by argument, becomes a far more dangerous tyranny when it becomes public property . . . even in England, hypotheses that have been current for some years are represented not as hypotheses, but as ascertained facts of modern scholarship.

—*SLS*, 46

Science

Science has an honourable mission, but it is not that of moulding the whole character of a civilization. It can show us the means to acquire a given end—as, for example, to travel at three hundred miles an hour, or to destroy a city with poison rays, or to breed dogs that will walk on their hind legs; but it can tell us nothing about the value of the end proposed, and humanity, to the last, will remain free to decide what ends it thinks admirable. This, as a rule, scientists recognize; nor do they feel that a slight has been put on their profession when it is mentioned. But of these modern priests of science I am more doubtful; they mean business, and they talk the language of fanaticism. It may be some day they will issue a challenge, which humanity, I hope, will not be slow to accept.

—*BCM*, 275

Science seconds our efforts, by inventing fresh ways of saving people's lives—except in war time, when it falls to quite as willingly to invent fresh ways of destroying them.

—*SAF,* 114

Science (Modern)

I think it is true to say that "Science", when it first began to argue self-consciously and to question older beliefs, hoped to dispel the foggy clouds of religious illusion by penetrating them with the clear light of reason; only make the facts plain, impart to the man in the street the knowledge which lay at the disposal of the man in the laboratory, and the public would find itself too clear-headed, too sophisticated, to believe. The aim of the omniscientists is, as far as I can see, the opposite; they want to convince the man in the street not of knowledge, but of ignorance. They want to confuse him with the riddles of science, not to enlighten him with its lucidity; so confused, will he be able any longer to trust his own judgment, to hold, therefore, any beliefs at all?

—*BCM,* 29–30

Einstein has proved that the universe is out of the straight, and Freud has proved that we never think what we think we are thinking, and Frazer or somebody has shown us that it was all a false alarm about God—what are we to do about it? We have got beyond the age of faith, beyond the age of hypothesis, into an age of pure assertion, without proof, in which we sit down and listen to the expert and wish we could learn to talk like that.

—*BCM,* 185

We should argue that, so long as science went hand in hand with common sense, *was,* in Huxley's phrase, organized common sense, it was impossible for us to doubt the laws which governed human thought. How could we doubt them, when they had achieved results so gratifyingly tangible? And these same laws could be used by the metaphysicians to infer the existence of a God of free will, of personal survival after death. But now that science, apparently following out these same laws, has fallen foul of common sense, finding it necessary to treat space as curved when we know it to be straight,

187

and make time an extra dimension of space, when we know it to be nothing of the kind, can we be certain any longer that the laws of human thought are valid?

—BCM, 187–88

Scientific Experts

Unless we are of those few who can claim to know everything about something, it only remains that we should pride ourselves on knowing something about everything. We must all have recourse to the little handbooks sooner or later. And the people whom I am criticizing, whose methods I am questioning . . . are not the people who derive their knowledge of most subjects from second-hand information . . . but people who select from the little handbooks those statements, those points of view which tell in favour of the thesis they want to establish, concealing any statements or points of view which tell in a contrary direction, and then serve up the whole to us as the best conclusions of modern research, disarming all opposition by appealing to the sacred name of science. It is these people I call the omniscientists.

—BCM, 21

Scientific Research

Research, at all times, has depended to some extent upon endowment, and it was not difficult to foresee what kind of research a medieval monarch would be inclined to endow in the circumstances. They set the alchemists to work at turning base metal into gold . . . then we all fell to laughing heartily at the stupid medieval fellows for imagining that you could turn one metal into another. Today, we are not so certain; the dream of the alchemists might become practicable . . . in our more fully equipped laboratories. . . . And if we still feel inclined to criticize those old kings for their commercial attitude towards research, let us chasten ourselves by reflecting how we did at last split the atom, and what use we made of it.

—GOD, 24–25

Scientism

It was still possible to see nothing absurd in Herbert Spencer's prediction "Progress is not an accident but a necessity—it is certain that man must become perfect", or to hope as Renan once hoped that Science "contains the future of humanity . . . and can take the place of religion". It is less easy for a modern Oxonian to see that the science which has given us the atom bomb can take the place of religion.

—DIF, 254

The Scottish

The Scottish garden is possibly a reflex of the Scottish character; the gaieties of life are there, but they must be relegated and enwalled, not suffered to interfere with life's purpose.

—SAF, 42

Scribes and Pharisees

What was wrong with the scribes and Pharisees wasn't so much that they didn't keep enough commandments as that they kept the commandments in a wrong spirit; in a niggling, haggling sort of spirit, determined to see how much they could indulge their own appetites and work off grudges against their neighbour without actually infringing the letter of the law. And that, our Lord tells us, is not the way to set about getting into the kingdom of heaven. The kingdom of heaven has its own court etiquette, and it is the law of love.

—LAY, 130–31

Scripture

We hold that Scripture is inspired, not in the metaphorical sense in which modern Protestants make that affirmation, nor yet in the limited sense that the Holy Ghost prevented the sacred authors from falling into error. We believe that the Scriptures have the Holy Ghost for their Author.

—DIF, 92

You destroy all value in the Scriptures as an independent source of certainty if you recognize their utterances as certain only where they overlap with the dogmas of the Church. If any part of the canonical Scriptures is to be regarded as immune from error *in its own right,* then the whole of them must be so regarded. You cannot, like Luther, declare St. James to be "an epistle of straw"; it must be as true as Galatians.

—*DIF,* 94

Pre-Reformation heresy was not condemned to sit at the feet of the pundit; each man adorned the sacred text with his own footnotes, and it may be presumed that the elusive quality of the old heterodoxies, both in England and abroad, was due in great measure to this complete freedom of interpretation.

—*EN,* 115

Either testament was sealed with blood; the old, when Moses sprinkled the document which enshrined it, the new, when those red drops trickled down the upright wooden beam. The new covenant has the cross for its parchment, blood for its ink.

—*PAS,* 508

Self-analysis

To make of yourself an object external to yourself is to encourage in yourself habits of posing, . . . of speculating over the figure you cut before the world; it may be of advantage in the literary profession to acquire such habits; in life it is a permanent nuisance. Children detected in the habit should certainly be smacked.

—*SPI,* 10

Self-assertion

Rooted deep in our nature, mysteriously prolific, spreading out in a network of subtle ramifications, lies the instinct of self-assertion. You see it in its crudest form in children, that desire to show off, to be thought important . . . we are compelled by the conventions of society to cover it up and pretend it is not there. But we know that it is there; how few people there are that can take it well, even outwardly, when their advice is not asked for, or is asked for and not taken . . . if we find such feelings are often with us; they are common enough . . . in the life of any moderately good Christian . . . they are perhaps the surest sign which could be given us, that we are not saints.

—PAS, 245–46

Selfishness

There are still ten people who say please for every one that says thank you.

—UAS, 374

Sermon on the Mount

It is not meant to be a social program; it is a message, primarily, to the individual Christian soul.

—PAS, 66

Simplicity

The whole idea of the Spiritual Childhood is that we shouldn't just be innocent, as children are; we should be simple with the simplicity of children.

—OCC, 91

Sin

There *are* mortal sins. Four hundred years ago, when the Reformation movement had got going, it was difficult to persuade people that any sins were venial; now, it is difficult to persuade them that any sins are mortal.

—HS, 169

Sin surely is rebellion, and the deliberateness of the rebellion is the measure of the sin's gravity.

—LIT, 56

Because all our worst sins take their origin in pride, the penance we are to offer—we moderns at least—must be prefaced by the mortification of reminding ourselves, what and whence we are.

—OCC, 89

We conceive of sin as a debt, as something demanding repayment, precisely in order to emphasize the fact that there is something in the eternal order of things which has been put out of joint by our sinful action, and the eternal order of things demands restitution: The penitent, after he has received Sacramental Absolution, though his soul is at the moment as completely in a state of grace . . . nevertheless owes to the offended Justice a penance which he must needs perform.

—SLS, 165

When you and I, by giving deliberate consent to a mortal sin, repeat in our lives the guilt of Calvary . . . we too have our Judas, our Caiaphas, our Pilate, to reckon with. . . . Your Judas is the occasion of sin. . . . Your Caiaphas is passion. . . . your Pilate is, practical reason . . . your reason gives way to consent. . . . And with that the decree is signed . . . you have pierced the heart of Christ. You are Judas, Caiaphas, and Pilate in one, if you have the heart to re-write that tragedy in your own name.

—UAS, 386–87

Sin (Original)

Original sin is the only key which fits the whole puzzle of existence.

—EN, 202

It would save a deal of trouble if we all agreed to call Original Sin Original Guilt. Because sin, in the mind of the common man, is something which he commits himself; whereas guilt is something he may get involved in through no fault of his own.

—HS, 164

Sinners

We think of the sinners who have been converted by coming in contact with the great saints, and seeing miracles done by them; or we think of the instances in which God has pulled up a sinner and drawn him to penance by some providence that struck across his life; and how we wish that that particular sinner, in whom we are so interested, could be given the same chance of restoration! And the answer is, *They have Moses and the prophets:* the sinner has sufficient grace.

—*PAS*, 116

"There shall be joy in heaven upon one sinner that doth penance, more than upon ninety-nine just who need not penance." That, surely, is a curious point of view. Are we to suppose that our Lord is giving countenance here to the illusion of those Protestants who will tell you that the forgiven sinner is a finer character than the soul that has kept its first innocence; that Mary Magdalen should claim higher honours than Mary the Mother of God?

—*PAS*, 126

That the holiest Church should produce the greatest sinners is but the natural application of the principle that the corruption of the best is the worst.

—*UAS*, 63

Slavery

It was only by slow degrees, and with notable set-backs, that St Paul's vision of "no more slave and freeman" came on to the statute-book. Even in the eighteenth century . . . so great a Christian as George Whitefield could own slaves, and could defend the system. But as and when the reform came about, it was the Christian tradition that moved men's consciences. At the back of their minds was the picture of a cold stable in the darkness of midnight, and God taking upon himself the nature of a slave for our sakes.

—*PAS*, 365

Socialism

More and more, as the beneficent schemes of our modern legislators take effect, the poor man is being reduced to the status of a bewildered slave. To help him understand and assert his own rights may, in the years that are coming, be a very important exercise of Christian charity.

—OCC, 234

The theologians will distinguish for you between *libertas a necessitate* and *libertas a coactione;* and it's a plain fact of human nature that people worry less about the pleasures they can't afford than about the pleasures which are forbidden them. More and more we find we've got to have *permits* for doing this and that, appeal to a tribunal before a certain date if we don't want this and that to happen in our back garden.

—OCC, 278

Social Reform

It is quite true that the Catholic Church has never made social reform the first plank in her programme; you might say that where she leavens society she always does so in a fit of absence of mind. Her message has always been addressed to the individual soul, rather than to the political community.

—UAS, 118

The social influence of the Church is in reality a by-product of her activity; it is not her life. Her business, ultimately, is with the individual soul, and the promises by which she lives are not limited within these narrow horizons.

—UAS, 121

Social Science

You cannot experiment, properly speaking, in matters of historical criticism, because your facts lie in the past; you can only make fresh observations, and the volume of possible fresh observations diminishes with research. Nor yet in anthropology, for you cannot isolate man in the mass and put him under the microscope. Nor yet in psychology, because the human mind cannot be seen working under test conditions except when it is reduced to an abnormal state; by drugs, for example, or by hypnotism. Accordingly, all the more important suggestions made in these fields are, and must remain, untested hypotheses; they are displaced, when they are displaced, by fresh theories based on observation, not by a strict method of proof.

$-BCM$, 58

Social Science Experts

The logical issue of our present tendencies, in political life, is a subservience to the expert more complete than the subservience of our ancestors to their Whig overlords in the early eighteenth century.

$-BCM$, 11

"Son of Man"

If you knew nothing about the Pope except that he called himself the slave of the slaves of God, you could infer quite easily that he regarded himself as the top man in Christendom, or he wouldn't have used such terms in describing himself. In the same way, you can give a good guess that our Lord wouldn't have been at such pains to call himself the Son of Man if he had not claimed to be something more than man when he did so.

$-UAS$, 35

It was probably a title connected in Jewish minds with the idea of the Messiah; and [Jesus] himself talks freely about the day when the Son of Man will come in judgment. But I think he showed a preference for that title just because it emphasized his humanity; and what was the point of emphasizing his humanity unless he were something more than an ordinary human being?

$-UAS$, 35

Sordidness

What is sordid in us is what we ourselves would be ashamed of if it came to light. When you are moved by jealousy to detract from the praises of some rival, that is sordid. When you grudge somebody the help he might

195

expect of you, just because he is a bore and uncongenial to you, that is sordid.

—LAY, 61

Souls

Probably one reason why some of the omniscientists—Mr Mencken, for example—are so keen to see synthetic life produced is that they imagine it would destroy an argument for the immortality of the soul; if life can be manufactured, why should it not be annihilated? But it is hardly necessary to point out that Christianity does not associate immortality with the possession of life, or even of conscious life, but with the possession of a rational soul.

—BCM, 267–68

Two sentiments may be expected to struggle for the mastery in a soul which has begun to turn towards God, the humility which would ask him for everything, and the generosity which would ask him for nothing.

—EN, 255

We are, as a matter of fact, intellectual souls; and those souls, our religion assures us, are immortal. But once we begin to think about ourselves as immortal souls, we are inclined to grow self-important and put on airs about it. So the first way in which we are encouraged to humiliate ourselves . . . is to remember (what is quite equally true) that we are dust—lumps of matter lying about for no very obvious reason in a world which is as material as ourselves.

—LAY, 14–15

You want to love souls; if you do not love souls, you will be hard put to it, in a world of so many temptations, to save your own.

—OCC, 41

Only God foreknows the souls that are his; it is not for us to say this man is saved, or that lost.

—PAS, 88

You think of your own soul, only one among . . . millions, and among all those millions so little distinguished by really vivid faith, by really generous love, by real intimacy with the things of eternity; can it really be, you ask yourself, that he cares for me? Just that little circle of friends he had while he lived on earth . . . for them, perhaps, he did care . . . when he prayed on the mountain-side or agonized in Gethsemani. But did that human regard of his extend now to all the souls existing now, all those millions, and among those millions does it extend to me? That is the doubt, the scruple, which the Blessed Sacrament sets aside for us.

—PAS, 303

The more a soul loves, the more it realizes its own sins; the more it realizes its own sins, the more it loves.

—UAS, 396

Spiritualism

I am going to take an interest in Spiritualism when the spirits can manage to produce a poem that is worth reading, or a statement that is not obvious, or a truth we did not know before which afterwards is verified. Meanwhile I doubt the source because I doubt the stream. We can call spirits from the vasty deep, and they will come when we do call for them. Having come, they assure us in sepulchral tones that honesty is the best policy.

—CAL, 190

Standards

That the true way of judging between us and our ancestors is not to call in a third party, but to compare both them and ourselves with an ideal standard. You must have your ideal first, abstracting as far as you can from all the prepossessions of your own world and century, and then you can judge both worlds by comparison with it.

—SAF, 32

God, not man, must be the measure of the Universe, must be the standard by which we are to judge all our experience. If we make man the centre of all our experience, then the riddle of existence becomes insoluble, and we had far better give it up.

—UAS, 15

If we ourselves have no abiding standard of right and wrong, if we ourselves have no clear idea of what the Christian revelation is, then it is much better to leave the unfortunate heathen alone. The morality of Confucius is at least definite. The creed of Mumbo-jumbo is at least consistent.

—UAS, 497

The State

There is a tendency for the State to assume greater and greater powers over the life of the individual citizen. It is, and is going to be, essentially the debate of our time how much and how far you may rightly sacrifice the freedom of the individual to the interests, real or imagined, of the whole community; and possibly, of the whole community as it will be a hundred years hence.

—OCC, 265

There's only one definition I know for it—a nation without a soul.

—UAS, 330

State Compulsion

There is a streak in us that dislikes State-managed concerns; it has long been possible for any mother to have her child brought up at the public expense, by depositing it on the doorstep of the nearest foundling home, but it only happens in unfortunate cases; and people still starve in a slum rather than live in a workhouse. But there is the possibility of State compulsion, I shall be reminded. That is true, but recent experiments in Prohibition do not suggest that it is easy for a public authority to alter violently the habits of a nation. And, of course, there is the Church. . . . It is an odd fact that a believer can always imagine the future more easily than an unbeliever. For the latter must be at pains to assume the disappearance of religion; the former is not bigoted enough to assume the disappearance of irreligion.

—BCM, 245–46

Suffering

There is a pain that kills and a pain that heals, and suffering comes to our lives for us to make use of it in which way we will. If we have learned in all our adversities, in sickness, in sorrow, in bereavement, in anxiety, in desolation, yes, even in doubts and scruples, to unite ourselves with his Passion, ours is the pain that heals: the more to suffer, the more to offer, that is the first principle of the Christian medicine.

—PAS, 86

In a word, suffering of some kind is the badge of the Christian profession, the accolade of the Christian knighthood. Suffering, to be sure, is the common lot of mortality, but Christians—I mean good Christians—will suffer more than their neighbours, because they are less indulgent to themselves, less sparing of their personal comfort, more sensitive to the needs of others.

—PAS, 197

Suffering, as we see it in this world, must be the wiping out of a debt; otherwise we should go mad with thinking of it, so unevenly distributed. If some of us have to suffer so much more than most of us, there must be compensation for that in the world to come. If you will not grant me that, then I will go out into the street with the atheists and rail at my God. That is our great comfort in this world; if some of us suffer so much more than most of us, there is compensation for it in another world.

—PAS, 466

Suffering for Christ

Suffering was to mean henceforth not, what it had always meant hitherto, something negative, sitting still and waiting for things to happen to you, the opposite of action, but something positive, the identification in will of the sinful and sin-laden victim with the Justice of God manifested in punishment.

—LAY, 74

The Supernatural

Christians adhere to God by faith, hope and charity. That is, they believe in the existence of a supernatural world; they conceive of the supernatural world as having its own purposes which are being worked out, obscurely to us, on this makeshift scene of time ... if you will, Christians believe in a God of whom St. Paul said, "Of him, and through him, and to him are all things." His existence gives our existence its explanation, tells us how we got here; its meaning tells us why things work out just so; its purpose tells us what we are here for. Notoriously, that explanation is given only on general lines; believe in God, and existence is still a riddle, faith is still needed if we are to hold that all is for the best; ... in the main we can be content; and those to whom the sense of God's existence is most vivid, holy people, seem to achieve both a lightness of heart and a lightness of touch which indicates that their lives are integrated: they are no longer worrying about the ultimate things.

$-GOD$, 10

Supernaturalists

The ultrasupernaturalist faced with a moral problem believes that the solution is given to him directly by the voice of God, and from that arbitrament there is no appeal.

$-EN$, 365

T

Teachers

The influence of the teacher is restricted to a few; and of those few, only a minority, at the best, do justice to the pains he took over them.

—OCC, 400

Technology

The mechanized world in which we live, eating eggs that come out of a tin, with unpiloted aeroplanes droning overhead, seems to have put us at the mercy of our own inventions; the machinery we created to be a useful servant has become a pitiless master.

—OCC, 54

Temperament

If, then, you are the sort of happy-go-lucky person whom the world calls "good-natured", then your nature wants watching; and probably it will need rules, irritating and cramping in themselves, while you are about it. Quite a lot of people, for instance, at least when they are in company where it is dangerous to let their tongues run away with them, would do well to count ten before they speak. If and so far as a man has the opposite temperament, the wizened, cautious, diffident temperament, it is doubtful if rules were meant for him. If he is to live by rules at all, let them be such as to counteract his poverty of nature, not to drive it deeper in. Some of us could afford to have this rule, where no sin or scandal is concerned—always to go by the first thought, and disregard the second. But this is heroic advice; few people are capable of profiting by it.

—LIG, 118

Temptation

Examine yourself to find, not the sin you most often commit, but the thing in your life which counts for most next to your religion, the thing which is more likely than anything else to count for even more than your religion. And then imagine to yourself what would happen if a strong temptation came across your path in that very matter. . . . Imagine the worst that could happen, and then tell God that, happen what may, he comes first.

—PAS, 165

Tertullian

It is difficult for us to imagine what a shock must have been given to the tender frame of second-century Christianity by the lapse of Tertullian, its great apologist, into Montanism. It was as if Newman had joined the Salvation Army.

—EN, 33

To me he is the born arguer, who talks himself, rather than thinks himself, into extreme positions, and is too dazzled by his own eloquence to recede from them.

—EN, 45

Theologians (Modern)

While theologians are trying desperately to reduce Christianity to those elements which it affirms in common with other religions, the really modern cry is to know wherein it differs from other religions . . . worst of all, when the enquirer goes to Church, to learn from the accredited teachers of our Religion what is expected of him, he finds in a hundred churches a hundred different standards upheld, till he begins to wonder what can possibly be made of a system whose apologists are so Protean.

—SLS, 14

The modern theologian is a Futurist in a very real sense. The future of the world and of the Church is ... very different from anything forecast by the Prophet of Nazareth. The signs of ... the Second Coming are found not in wars and rumours of wars, but in a programme of universal peace; not in famines and pestilences, but in the ... improvement of hospitals. He cannot believe that many shall be offended, because Christianity is to be purged of all that could possibly offend ... or that the love of many shall wax cold, because charity is soon to be universal and dominant. He looks forward to a completion, *in this world,* of the design of our creation; not to a sudden interruption of the process.

—*SLS,* 113

Theology (Modern)

If we are to have a shop-window theology, a theology which we are to present to the waverer for his acceptance, it is before all things necessary that it should be lucid.

—*SLS,* 15

Today

To-day is unique; it has never happened before, it can never happen again. For one moment it is all-important, fills the stage; tomorrow it will have taken its place in the unreal pageant of dead yesterdays. It has a significance, then, all its own; but this significance belongs to it because it is related to a series. We may think of it as the beginning of a series, the first day of a new departure in our lives. Or we may think of it as one day among others, with the same duties, cares, temptations as the others. Or we may think of it as the last of a series; one to-day will be the last of all our to-days, with eternity for its infinite tomorrow, and it may be this.

—*PL,* 169

Tongues

I do not mean to deny the existence of glossolaly. ... To speak with tongues you had never learned was, and is, a recognized symptom in cases of alleged diabolical possession. What does not appear is that it was ever claimed, at least on a large scale, as a symptom of divine inspiration, until the end of the

203

seventeenth century . . . among the appellant (but still nominally Catholic) Jansenists.

—EN, 551

Tradition

A rule may be interpreted; a tradition must be preserved or perish.

—OCC, 77

Translators

A scholar here, a poet there, who thinks it is time he produced the absolutely perfect rendering of *Persicos odi,* or of *Animula vagula, blandula.* He works neither for fame nor for reward; he has simply taken a bet with himself, as it were, that the thing can be done, and cannot sleep sound till he has done it.

—LIT, 36–37

I have urged that the translator's business is to recondition, as often as not, whole sentences, so as to allow for the characteristic emphasis of his own language. I have urged that it is his business to transpose whole phrases, so as to reduce them to the equivalent idiom of his own language.

—TOT, 11

Transubstantiation

In this mystery of transubstantiation, he has broken into the very heart of nature, and has separated from one another in reality two elements which we find it difficult to separate even in thought, the inner substance of things from those outward manifestations of it which make it known to our senses . . . call to your aid all the resources of science, and flood it with a light stronger than human eyes can bear to look upon, still that white disc will be nothing better than a dark veil, hiding the ineffable light of glory which shines in and through the substance of Christ's ascended body.

—PAS, 205

The Trinity (Huxley's Modern Explanation)

Professor Huxley will have no Veiled Being; he will stick to concrete realities. And his statement of the Nicene doctrine might *well* go down to history as one of the curiosities of literature. Here it is, in his own summary (pp. 61, 62): "As I see it broadly, God the Father is a personification of the forces of non-human Nature; God the Holy Ghost represents all ideals; and God the Son personifies human nature at its highest, as actually incarnate in bodies and organized in minds, bridging the gulf between the other two, and between each of them and everyday human life. And the unity of the three persons as One God represents the fact that all these aspects of reality are inextricably connected." In fact, his trinity consists of the real, the human mind and the ideal. That, doubtless, is what the early Fathers would have meant if they had had the advantage of a scientific education—three persons in no God.

—BCM, 89

Truth

The motto on Cardinal Newman's tomb ought to be the funeral motto of every Catholic, *Ex umbris et imaginibus in veritatem,* Out of shadows and appearances into the truth.

—PAS, 258

Truth, once it is rightly apprehended, has a compelling power over men's hearts; they must needs assert and defend what they know to be the truth, or they would lose their birthright as men.

—PAS, 456

Twentieth Century

An age which had gone mad over a hundred speculative fanaticisms, whose prophets had saturated the public.

—LIT, 157

Tyranny

Where a nation loses sight of God, it tends to deify man; you will read that lesson without difficulty in the story of tyrannies, whether they be ancient or modern.

—OCC, 211

Tyrants and Laughter

The tyrant may arm himself in triple mail, may surround himself with bodyguards, may sow his kingdom with a hedge of spies, so that free speech is crushed and criticism muzzled. Nay, worse, he may so debauch the consciences of his subjects with false history and with sophistical argument that they come to believe him the thing he gives himself out for, a creature half-divine, a heaven-sent deliverer. One thing there is that he still fears; one anxiety still bids him turn this way and that to scan the faces of his slaves. He is afraid of laughter. The satirist stands there, like the little child, in the procession when the Emperor walked through the capital in his famous new clothes; his is the tiny voice that interprets the consciousness of a thousand onlookers: "But, Mother, he has no clothes on at all!"

—ESS, 35–36

U

Undergraduates

It is the nature of the undergraduate to discuss all things in heaven and earth with the utmost seriousness and sometimes with very slight information.

—*UAS*, 128

The Universe

I deny that the universe loves all its children equally, because I know that the universe has no children, and that it does not "love" anyone or anything at all. I am not going to assume that it "cherishes" anything; it does not devote its life to anybody, nor has it in any intelligible sense a "life" to devote. And I see no use in speculating what the universe would do if it wrote its memories, because I know that it can neither read nor write. It is because man can love, and cherish, and devote himself, and write, and do all those things which the universe cannot, that I am prepared not merely to regard him as the most important thing in the universe, but to deny that (apart from theology) there could be any such thing as "importance" in the universe if man did not exist.

—*BCM*, 215

I find it quite impossible to conceive this amorphous lump which we call the Universe either as having existed from all time, or as having brought itself into existence: I demand a Personality behind the scenes.

—*SLS*, 202

Utopia

Optimism is at a discount; men clamour, not for happiness, but for security, and when a ship's passengers demand life-belts rather than cabins, it is idle to pretend there is no danger of foundering. Heaven knows, there are more factors than one contributing to our present atmosphere of panic. But the imagination is most easily dominated by the threat of the Atom, the thing which has peeped out at us so suddenly and so enigmatically; flashed its message to us with a brightness above the brightness of the sun. Are we really expected to go on bothering about Utopia, when we have to allow for the possibility that modern weapons, used indiscriminately, might make of the world a Utopia in the literal sense, a Nowhere?

—*GOD*, 116–17

V

Values

Aesthetic values, intellectual values, patriotic values—all these have their part on the world's stage; but they are only supers; their rôle is only to make sham conversation in the background. The celestial limelight is thrown full on man's interior life; only the contemplation of this thrills the Angelic court with expectation.

—SLS, 219

Vows

Vows—what a significant part they have played, what a tragic part, often, they have played in human history! Rash vows, broken vows, vows directed to an evil end and so made dishonourable in the keeping—how much safer, in some ways, the world would be without them! Yet man claims obstinately the right to engage himself, the liberty of signing away his own liberty. For this reason: that the mood of the moment, the mood in which he is carried away out of himself, is sometimes, he feels, the mood in which he is most truly himself, and he does not trust it to last.

—OCC, 320

W

Walking

I know some people think that a walk is the proper way to talk a thing over, dons especially, but then they go for the same walk every day, and know it as a horse in a milk-cart knows its rounds. But for me, scenery spoils thought, and thought scenery; and when I come back from a walk on which I have talked seriously, I am a limp rag as the result of using up body-tissues and mind-tissues at once.

—*SAF*, 39

War

We will not let ourselves be blinded by the lure of worldly success so as to forget that the true statesmanship is exercised in the council chamber, and the true warfare fought on the battlefield of the human soul.

—*OCC*, 26

War divides men's souls from their bodies.

—*PAS*, 211

War Crimes

I conceive that if the enemy begin shooting prisoners-of-war you may rightly threaten to do the same; though even so you are letting down the standards of civilization. But if you carry your threat into effect, you are doing precisely what the Germans did when they shot civilian hostages as reprisals for the assassination of their own jacks-in-office. To shoot, in cold blood, the unarmed man who is not himself guilty of any offence is not simply killing, it is murder; you cannot claim the privilege of belligerency, for war itself has no such usage. And war must have usages to justify it, if it is to be justified at all.

−GOD, 70

Warfare (Atomic)

Atomic energy has been manifested to us, so far, only as an instrument of death; and the bomb (like all explosive weapons, but on a scale hitherto unimaginable) is a weapon in the hands of tyranny. It is suited to the needs of a world in which you no longer count heads to save breaking them, but blow off heads to save the trouble of counting them.

−GOD, 86

H. G. Wells' *Outline of History*

It all began, in a sense, with Mr Wells's *Outline of History*. We knew Mr Wells for a man who could turn his hand to anything, who, by his uncanny literary gift, could make any sort of improbability seem probable, in the manner of Jules Verne. But we had not pictured him as a historian. And then the book came out, and we realized that his treatment of his subject did not really need any knowledge of history. . . . It had nothing to do with that interplay of motive and destiny which lends human history its interest. It was "history" in the sense in which men will write a history of the pig. . . . And the ingredients which went into the pot were biology, palaeontology, anthropology—all the stuff which we could have got up equally well for ourselves out of the handbooks, only we should not have had the cleverness to make it so newsy and so saleable. It was a phantasia, history as Mr Wells wanted us to see it, with materials drawn from so wide a range of sources that . . . he could always find some point of view, some opinion, which favoured his own thesis.

−BCM, 21−22

Wesley, John

Wesley himself, who gave up tea by way of setting a good example to the poor, was perhaps less consistent in the matter of celibacy; four days after deciding to marry, he met the single men and urged them to remain single for the kingdom of Heaven's sake, 'except where a particular case might be an exception to the general rule'.

—*EN*, 444

It would be hard to find another man so famous whose works are less generally read.

—*EN*, 446–47

From its very nature his movement attracted the attention and often the sympathies of the queer people in the world, borderline cases who would have been written down by anybody except Wesley as hysterical patients at best, and probably lunatics.

—*EN*, 543

Wesley had the mind of a Jesuit and the morals of a Jansenist.

—*EN*, 493

Wesleyan Movement

Lest any reader ... exclaim in bewilderment over the spiritual phenomena of the Wesleyan movement, asking how such things could happen in the England of Dr Johnson, it will not be out of place to have reminded him that still more extraordinary things had been happening in the France of Bayle, and Diderot, and Voltaire.

—*EN*, 388

Westminster Abbey

That strange mausoleum of nine hundred years of English history which is neither church nor cathedral, because it is too proud to be either.

—OCC, 24

Wigs and the Eighteenth Century

I believe we are frightened of the eighteenth century because it wore wigs. There is something pontifical about the wig: judges still wear it, in order to convince us that they are endowed with superhuman wisdom; and the Bishops ought never to have abandoned it, for we have none of us believed a word they said since.

—SAF, 27

Wisdom

The Book of Wisdom! It is a deliberate paradox, for the word "wise" in Scriptural language has often the sense of crafty; the unjust steward is commended because he acted wisely, and the children of this world in their generation are wiser than the children of light. But there is a wisdom which somehow these innocent, gullible, ineffective, open-handed simpletons have got hold of, while these smart, up-to-date, very much alive men of business have missed it. Now, which is right?

—OCC, 26

Wit

Wit demands a soil of civilisation to grow in; it will not spring up self-sown, like . . . ale-house humour.

—LIT, 83

There is a subtle quality about the really great wits which is not of the period to which they belong. Not in the sense that they are misfits, that they are unrepresentative of their periods. . . . Rather in the sense that they overflow the common water-courses, and leave a saline deposit for after ages to admire.

—LIT, 83

Woman

Woman (St Paul tells us elsewhere), although she was the last to be created and the first to fall into sin, is to find her salvation in the great Child-bearing;[1] after the events of Christmas Day, she can never be thought of as a mere chattel for man's use; she is a free being, apt for partnership with man.

—PAS, 365

Words

Words are born and die; they live only so long as they have an important errand to fulfil, by expressing what needs expression.

—EN, 6

Words are not coins, dead things whose value can be mathematically computed. You cannot quote an exact English equivalent for a French word, as you might quote an exact English equivalent for a French coin. Words are living things, full of shades of meaning, full of associations; and, what is more, they are apt to change their significance from one generation to the next. The translator who understands his job feels, constantly, like Alice in Wonderland trying to play croquet with flamingoes for mallets and hedgehogs for balls; words are for ever eluding his grasp.

—TOT, 13

Work

Can we not learn to be content with the work, however humble its sphere may be, which God has given us to do; content to be overlooked and passed by, to have our opinion disregarded, to be left out in the cold?

—OCC, 143–44

[1] 1 Tim 2:13–15.

The World

The world is never at peace.

—OCC, 266

If Art, and Science, and Nationality, and all else that the world treasures, were drowned in the depths of the sea, the ultimate value of life would remain unaffected. Of which it has been said, Fear God, and keep his commandments, for this is the whole duty of Man.

—SLS, 219

Wars or famines or pestilence ... have left the survivors uncertain of their prospects, uncertain of life itself. ... At such times, men have often turned to their religion with more ardour, have separated themselves from the world and gone to live as hermits or in the cloister, reminded at last that we have here no abiding city. ... It is not an illusion people get at such times that the world is transitory. Rather at such times they lose the illusion that the world is permanent. They realize more than at other times what is true at all times, that the whole of this visible creation is but a thin plank between us and eternity.

—PAS, 258–59

World (Modern)

Faithful Catholics, still more if you are preaching the Catholic religion, will be outlaws to some extent in the world of today, a world which tends more and more to banish religion from its speech and its thought.

—OCC, 42

The world is very old nowadays, and we are all very grown-up; you can buy the wisdom of the ages for a shilling on a bookstall; the newspapers fling problems at us, ... tell us to make money, and to want as much as possible. ... Conventions of civilization, the second servant and the fresh suit on Sundays and the latest fashion in hats and in eyebrows make life expensive for us and complicated. But ... is our world really a happy world? Can we look back at the age of St Francis without feeling something of

215

regret for our own childhood, ... when we see, in the house where we were brought up, the familiar passage that leads to the nursery door?

—*OCC,* 99

Our age, more than ever, is lost in admiration of man's greatness.

—*OCC,* 120

It is one of the few satisfactions you get out of living in times like these, that they help you to understand history. The emergence of the modern gangster-State has made it much easier.

—*OCC,* 137

The world is so full of anxiety about the present, of speculation about the future, that it has no time to waste, no tears to shed, over the ruined glories of the past.

—*OCC,* 160

Ever since Lowes Dickinson's *Greek View of Life* there has been a thin stream of books by dons trying to represent Greece and Rome, instead of Nazareth, as the true cradle of civilization, but its effect has been negligible. The modern world feels that it can manage to go pagan for itself, without any dons to show it how.

—*OCC,* 341–42

Our modern age, on the strength of rather moderate literary achievements, loves to proclaim itself an age of humanism. The spokesmen of such an age, at a hundred different angles, show themselves more than ever unfriendly to the whole idea of revealed religion. [But] the world, tired of listening to long wrangles between the philosophers, is coming to doubt whether the intellect is a competent judge of the living truth. Especially in matters of religion.

—*OCC,* 355

World-domination

World-domination, after all, belongs not to the cause which has right on its side, but to the cause which has the best-equipped laboratories on its side.

—GOD, 95

X Y Z

Youth

Youth will be always daring, always making experiments; it finds something depressing about last year's model.

— OCC, 268

Youth will fling itself into any ambition, however trumpery, as if with a lifetime's ardour; we burn for a cause, or live for an ambition, as if nothing else mattered.

— PAS, 286

BIBLIOGRAPHY OF RONALD KNOX WORKS CITED WITH ABBREVIATIONS

BAR:	*Barchester Pilgrimage.* New York: Sheed and Ward, 1936.
BCM:	*Broadcast Minds.* London: Sheed and Ward, 1932.
CAL:	*Caliban in Grub Street.* London: Sheed and Ward, 1931.
DIF:	*Difficulties,* by Ronald Knox and Arnold Lunn. London: Eyre and Spottiswoode, 1932.
EN:	*Enthusiasm.* London: Oxford University Press, 1950.
ESS:	*Essays in Satire.* London: Sheed and Ward, 1930.
GOD:	*God and the Atom.* New York: Sheed and Ward, 1946.
HS:	*The Hidden Stream.* London: Burns and Oates, 1952.
ISG:	*In Soft Garments.* New York: Burns and Oates, 1942.
LAY:	*The Laymen and His Conscience.* New York: Sheed and Ward, 1961.
LDD:	*Let Dons Delight.* London: Sheed and Ward, 1939.
LIG:	*Lightning Meditations.* New York: Sheed and Ward, 1959.
LIT:	*Literary Distractions.* New York: Sheed and Ward, 1958.
OCC:	*Occasional Sermons.* New York: Sheed and Ward, 1960.
OR:	*Off the Record.* New York: Sheed and Ward, 1954.
OTO:	*Other Eyes than Ours.* London: Methuen and Co., 1926.
PAS:	*The Pastoral Sermons.* New York: Sheed and Ward, 1960.
PL:	*The Priestly Life.* New York: Sheed and Ward, 1958.
RFP:	*A Retreat for Priests.* New York: Sheed and Ward, 1959.
SAF:	*Sanctions: A Frivolity.* London: Sheed and Ward, 1932.
SLS:	*Some Loose Stones.* London: Longmans Green and Co., 1913.
SPI:	*A Spiritual Aeneid.* New York: Sheed and Ward, 1958.
TOT:	*Trials of a Translator.* New York: Sheed and Ward, 1949.
UAS:	*University and Anglican Sermons.* London: Burns and Oates, 1963.

INDEX OF SOURCES

INDEX OF TOPICS

George J. Marlin serves as Executive Director of The Port Authority of New York and New Jersey, President of the Port Authority Trans Hudson Corporation and President of the Newark Legal Center.

Prior to his appointment he spent seventeen years in the municipal finance industry.

Mr. Marlin has co-authored with Joe Mysak *The Guidebook to Municipal Bonds: The History, the Industry, the Mechanics.* He is a general editor of *The Collected Works of G. K. Chesterton* and editor of *The Quotable Chesterton, More Quotable Chesterton, The Quotable Fulton Sheen* and *The Quotable Paul Johnson.* His articles have appeared in numerous periodicals including *National Review, Crisis, The Chesterton Review, Fidelity, Credit Markets, Reflections, Muniweek,* and *The Wanderer.* A frequent contributor to *The Bond Buyer,* Mr. Marlin has written extensively on New York's finances and politics.

Richard P. Rabatin, a professional musician, resides in Stony Brook, New York. Born in 1950, Mr. Rabatin received his undergraduate degree in political science from the State University of New York at Stony Brook. He received his Master's Degree at Fordham University in political science, and he studied musical composition at Berklee College of Music in Boston. Mr. Rabatin is also a general editor of *The Collected Works of G.K. Chesterton* and an editor of *The Quotable Chesterton, More Quotable Chesterton* and *The Quotable Fulton Sheen.*

John L. Swan is a partner in the community relations firm Institutional Planning and Development Corporation. He was formerly associated with the National Broadcasting Corporation and the American Cancer Society. Mr. Swan, a lifelong resident of New York City, is also a general editor of *The Collected Works of G.K. Chesterton* and an editor of *The Quotable Chesterton, More Quotable Chesterton* and *The Quotable Fulton Sheen.*

George W. Rutler is a priest of the Archdiocese of New York. A noted preacher and author, Father Rutler's latest book is *The Seven Ages of Man.*